"In today's competitive environment it's harder than ever for businesses and salespeople to create sizeable profits. If you want your business to stand out from your competitors, you need a fresh approach and Johnson's game plan for salespeople and business managers really works. Not only can she explain these concepts in a compelling way, but by applying these concepts and succeeding, she has done it herself!"

–Gord Huston, CEO Envision Financial, Langley, BC

*The Jalapeño Handshake* is an engaging read that uses illumination rather than retraining as the gateway to tap personal power and build trust. Anyone who finds themselves in a position where they need to sell their ideas, their products, or meet arbitrary sales objectives will find this book very inspiring, relevant, and .very practical."

–Denise R. Gabel \ Chief Innovation Officer \ Filene Research Institute

"Success in selling is the ability to truly understand our customers' needs, build a strong and trusting relationship with them and then show them how you can give them what they want and more". Drawing on her own experience and that of well known and respected leaders in their field, Lydia Johnson has managed to capture the essence of how to be successful in selling and life in general."

–Eitan Sharir, President Dynamic Achievement Group, Inc. and author of Activate Your Power

"The strategies in *The Jalapeno Handshake* are not only for salespeople or business managers, but for the rest of us as well. Johnson examines how we hold ourselves back, and how to harness the inner resources we need to achieve our goals."

–Peter Lee, Principal, Tekara Organizational Effectiveness Inc. Vancouver, BC

"Johnson shares simple strategies that will add value to any customer interaction. She shows us how to build strong relationships with our clients that will stand the test of time. Thanks for reminding us that it is the little things that can make a huge difference - thanks for putting things into perspective for us!"

–Kim Andres, Kim Andres Consulting

"Lydia's rich experience as a seasoned sales leader shines through on every page, as she lays out a holistic and practical handbook for growing sales in any industry. A must-read for emerging sales professionals, and a smart choice for experienced business developers looking to sharpen their edge. This is the straightforward, grounded guidance we all appreciate, because we can put the tools to work tomorrow morning."

–Ross Gilchrist, Leader / Strategic Design and Talent, The Next Institute

"If you would like your business to stand out from the competition, succeed beyond expectations and thrive during challenging times I highly recommend Lydia's book *The Jalapeno Handshake*."

–Peggy McColl, New York Times Best-Selling Author http://peggymccoll.com

"Lydia Johnson "talks her walk". The insight she shares in Jalapeño Handshake comes from her own top performance in business relationships. Lydia's invaluable lessons are ideal for anyone committed to achieving m ore."

–Candy Hodson Senior VP National Sales & Marketing, Black Press Media

"Johnson provides you with a complete set of tools to assist in cultivating strong business relationships. The rules have changed and in her book she illustrates many valuable strategies that enable us to be resilient in these challenging times."

–Alan Cline President/CEO 1-800-PLUMBING INC Phoenix, Arizona

"Customer-centric sales and service strategies and tactics are the life blood for building competitive, profitable success in business and life. Lydia Johnson is a practitioner-leader in this area and her book can help both businesses and individuals reach new levels of prosperity."

–P.A. (Pat) Palmer, Founder & CEO Where Eagles Soar Inc Markdale, ON

"Being a great business leader is about inspiring your staff as well as your customers. Johnson gives you the tools to do both! An excellent read for anyone who is looking to boost a business. *The Jalapeno Handshake* adds a little spice to stale sales tactics. This book is an engaging and insightful read for salespeople and business managers everywhere."

–Grace Pulver Management Consultant

"You never get a second chance to treat people right and it is vital to create an atmosphere of trust and integrity with both customers and employees. *The Jalapeño Handshake* is an excellent read for anyone who is looking to boost a business."

–Peter Reale Branch Manager Vancity - 4th Avenue Community Branch

"Every person has times when they're just plain HOT, and winning big feels easy. Lydia Johnson explains how to consciously create that! After reading *The Jalapeno Handshake* I'm able to flip switches that I never knew I had. My relationships and results are on the climb for sure."

–Chris Curran, author of *Leap Beyond Your Limits*

"As a successful executive with an impressive career background, Lydia writes from experience not opinion. Her thoughts are crafted from the school of hard knocks so you know when you're reading every page that she travelled the road and she's giving it to you straight. If you're trying to standout from the crowd, truly learn how to build effective long term business relationships, and become a "connector," this is the book for you."

–Mike Desjardins Driver (CEO), ViRTUS - Past President, Entrepreneurs' Organization - Vancouver Chapter Top 40 Under 40 Award Recipient

"Having worked with Lydia for 12 years, I witnessed her energy and great ability to sell. Lydia describes the techniques and little "tricks of the trade" that I am once again teaching. This book has been an enjoyable refresher for me and I know you will also enjoy it."

–Kevin J. Zakus, CEO BCCA  Employee Benefit Trust

THE Jalapeño
Handshake

THE **Jalapeño** HANDSHAKE

Strategies To **Heat Up** Your Business Relationships

# LYDIA JOHNSON

LIFESUCCESS PUBLISHING, LLC
8900 E. Pinnacle Peak Road, Suite D240
Scottsdale, AZ 85255

| | |
|---|---|
| Telephone: | 800.473.7134 |
| Fax: | 480.661.1014 |
| E-mail: | admin@lifesuccesspublishing.com |
| ISBN: | 978-1-59930-336-9 |

| | |
|---|---|
| Cover: | Eric Choi, LifeSuccess Publishing, LLC |
| Text: | Lloyd Arbour, LifeSuccess Publishing, LLC |
| Edit: | Publication Services Inc. |

COMPANIES, ORGANIZATIONS, INSTITUTIONS, AND INDUSTRY PUBLICATIONS. Quantity discounts are available on bulk purchases of this book for reselling, educational purposes, subscription incentives, gifts, sponsorship, or fundraising. Special books or book excerpts can also be created to fit specific needs such as private labeling with your logo on the cover and a message from a VIP printed inside. For more information, please contact our Special Sales Department at LifeSuccess Publishing, LLC.

Mixed Sources
Product group from well-managed forests and other controlled sources
www.fsc.org  Cert no. SW-COC-002283
© 1996 Forest Stewardship Council

# DEDICATION

To all those who are open minded, interested, and curious to learn.

To Aiden and Cadence, who remind me every day of life's endless possibilities. Thank you for believing and trusting. You fill my heart with pride, with love, and with great joy. Never stop being curious and never stop asking good questions. May you always learn, grow, and reach for your own stars.

# ) CONTENTS

# FOREWORD

One of the most difficult challenges facing the professional salesperson—facing *everyone*—is how to establish strong, lasting relationships. For the salesperson, professional survival depends on connecting with customers and maintaining those relationships. For non-salespeople, we count on our relationships in every aspect of our lives, with family, friends, and co-workers.

The message that Lydia Johnson offers in *The Jalapeño Handshake* is that each of us has the power and can develop the ability to create and develop the trust necessary to make powerful, high-quality relationships. The key is to act always with integrity and transparency, making yourself trustworthy—that is, *worthy* of another's trust—and setting the foundation for creating a great relationship.

With more than three decades of experience in sales and service, Lydia uses real examples to show how, by conquering our own fears and developing our own sense of personal responsibility, we are able to fully understand and grow the qualities in ourselves that we look for in others. Unless we know and understand our own minds, we can't develop the empathy we need to connect with other people.

*The Jalapeño Handshake* is a guide to lead you from the disappointments of flawed relationships—both professional and personal—that haven't worked out, to interactions with other people at a level you would never have thought possible. We all crave tight, strong attachments and friendships with others. Lydia Johnson points readers in the right direction, providing them with a virtual how-to in creating a happier, more fulfilling life that includes other people.

I challenge you to learn Lydia Johnson's tips and techniques, and apply them in your own life. Your relationships will be absolutely transformed.

–Candy Hodson
**Senior VP, National Sales & Marketing**
**Black Press Media**
**Surrey, BC**

# ) ACKNOWLEDGMENTS

I am very grateful for the many people in my life who cheered me on during this project. Your belief in me was inspiring and kept me moving. I'm so lucky to have you share this with me.

Thank you, Tracey and Chris, who are always there for me; and my friends who shared and cared…you were all fantastic to have on this journey: Debbie x 2, Denise, Eileen, Grace, Kenny, Marilyn, Maws, Mindy, Neil, Thomas.

I would like to thank the people who supported me in this journey. It's an honor to have shared this place in my life with you all. It's wonderful having your trust in my messages and teachings.

And thanks to my project team of Kyle, Veronica, and Wendy. You are the best!

"IF A PERSON WILL ADVANCE
CONFIDENTLY IN THE DIRECTION OF
THEIR DREAM AND ENDEAVOUR TO
LIVE THE LIFE THEY HAVE IMAGINED,
THEY WILL MEET WITH SUCCESS
UNEXPECTED IN COMMON HOURS."

–Henry David Thoreau

# ) INTRODUCTION

) The idea for the title of this book stemmed from an experience I had with my grandkids while on a family vacation in Mexico. Ages six and three, they had had little experience with the exotic, flavorful foods they encountered there. The kids were afraid of biting into a jalapeño that was going to burn their mouths. With every new dish, they would turn to Mom or Dad or me and ask, "Is it hot? Is it spicy?"

If we answered yes, they left it alone. If we said no, they dived in with enthusiasm, forks flying. They trusted us enough to know that they could count on our answers to guide them toward food that wouldn't be too hot and spicy for their young palates.

What do jalapeños and business relationships have in common anyway? When we think of jalapeños, we think of hot…very hot. We think of burning our mouths or our fingers. On the other hand, we also think of enhancing the flavors of our foods and the added kick of what can be tasted when we use chili peppers properly. They can be as wonderful on the one hand as they are perceived as dangerous on the other.

I come from the position that we are all in sales in one way or another. We sell each other on our everyday life ideas, from what movie to see to an idea for decorating a room, or to the writing of contracts for multimillion-dollar sales transactions. We all sell something sometime to someone, more often than we realize. It's that simple.

So although we are all in sales, many of us have chosen to make sales our profession. Sales professionals make or break business relationships.

Some are small, such as those with the local corner store, while others are between huge businesses that demand strong sales results. "Heating up" relationships in businesses of all sizes is what *The Jalapeño Handshake* is all about. Enhancing business relationships always starts with the value the salesperson brings to the business. It also starts with a company's value for how sales relationships are built. The magic is in the combination of both. That's what makes the relationship heat up!

For me, sales started with sponges—yes, sponges, of all things. Everyday, ordinary sponges…the kind that come in different colors and look like small bricks. Sponges were what kicked off my passion for sales. When I look at a sponge today, I'm still transported back to those roots.

You see, I was 12 years old and had just moved from Ontario, Canada, to the small east coast town of Glace Bay, Nova Scotia. My father was setting up a tire store in this new and, as it then seemed to me, very strange small town. I remember only wanting to be back with my friends in my old neighborhood 1,500 miles away.

But that was not going to be the case. My life changed in good ol' Glace Bay. Within a few days of arriving in our new town, after a two-day road trip with my parents and three of my five brothers, my father sat us all down and told us the reality of our new jobs, starting that afternoon. He said that he would put food on the table and a roof over our heads, and we were going to have to work for everything else we wanted or needed. Our jobs started a few hours later.

I was quite happy to have limited experience of the working world. At the time, the only job experience under my belt was snow removal in my old neighborhood during tough winters. I had made one dollar for every driveway I could make drivable for local neighbors, teachers, and "older" people. (Little did I know then that I would become one myself in a flash.) They were my target markets.

While still living in Ontario, I had also had the worldly working experience of filing my father's work orders from his service station sales into numeric order most work nights when he came home. I had had a whole three or so years' experience and had spent probably way too long organizing lots of piles of invoices so they were ready for whatever he would do with them. I never asked.

So when our father told us that we would be working and that our jobs started that same afternoon, we each looked around to determine who he might be talking to. Watching each of my brothers' faces—they were 11, 14, and 15—I saw that we were all shaken by this new reality of not only being in a new town at what seemed like the end of the world, but also having to earn some sort of a living. And so my sales career began…

Within a few weeks of becoming a near-expert on the cash register, making change, and learning more than I ever thought I'd want to learn about car parts, garden equipment, painting supplies, and hardware, I was presented with a storage and inventory problem.

My father had misordered sponges. Instead of receiving ten packages of sponges, which is what he thought he had ordered, we received ten *cases* of sponges, and each case contained ten packages. He had ordered ten times as many sponges than he had intended. We had a very small store with very limited space in the basement for storing inventory, and we were overrun with sponges—light, fun, colored sponges.

When he realized what he had done, he gave me the responsibility of getting rid of the sponges as fast as I could. I knew he didn't mean to give them away or throw them away; I needed to sell them.

So I began to think about sponges and what to do with them. I knew what our household used them for and then thought of anything else that could be cleaned with a good old sponge.

We had only one cash register, located close to the door, so I got to see everyone who left the store, whether they bought anything or not. As every customer checked out their purchases, I knew I had a captive audience. The challenge began!

No matter what they bought, they heard about the great use of sponges—washing the car (the obvious), the dog, the cat, the windows, the bathtub, the floors, the kids, the kitchen sink, the laundry room, and even an application behind furniture to protect the wall. I thought of every possible use for a sponge and every way I could introduce these useful ideas to our customers, and then simply asked for the business. Of course I didn't realize I was *asking for the business*. That I learned much later in my sales life.

A day or so later, my father became angry when he saw that there were no sponges displayed at my till. I said they were all gone, even the ones in the storage room. Shaking his head in disbelief, he checked the basement and couldn't find any sponges. He asked what I had done with them. Of course, my answer was the truth—I had sold them.

At that time, I realized that this thing called sales could be a lot of fun and was a fun challenge too. So I began trying it out with every customer I encountered. Whatever they were in the store for, I found a way to talk about some other product that they might need now or later. It was fun to be as crazy and creative as possible. I discovered that people loved hearing about something that could add value to their lives, in small ways or big ways. And so, my sales career and passion for sales began, all thanks to the sponges, those lovely multicolored, brick-shaped sponges that could be used on cars, cats, dogs, kitchens, bathrooms, floors, walls, and almost anything else.

More years than I care to admit have passed since those days. Many sales have taken place during that time, but I always remember sponges for the valuable lessons they taught me, which I have used over the years. You see, whether it is sponges or financial services, coffee or cars, new houses or anything else, sales makes the world go around.

If we didn't have people selling things, there would be lots of stuff on warehouse shelves, stuck in vast computer systems attached to some company's financial statements and not getting into the hands of buyers. Our economy would come to a grinding halt, and no one would be able to sponge-wash their car on a sunny Sunday, outside their new home, after enjoying a rich blend coffee while checking their investments in the financial section of the paper.

Sales connects us all to what we need or want in our lives. Salespeople help make those connections. The very best part of salespeople connecting others to what they need or want is building a trusted relationship with their buyers. It takes a level of trust similar to that which my grandchildren displayed in Mexico.

This is the ultimate power of sales. It makes everything easier and more meaningful for both buyer and seller. The relationship is almost a partnership. Sales is really service, in every sense, and as a relationship is developed, the service simply continues to evolve to new products or services. In fact, I believe you can't separate sales from service. They are inextricably intertwined. In order to do one well, you need to do the other.

Life stages create new buying needs and new selling opportunities. Being in a strong, trusted relationship means a customer and a sales expert grow that relationship together. Most of us can think of such a relationship, one that we know we can count on when we need honest buying advice and the straight goods on a product. We know who we can trust to serve us well.

Sadly, most of us also know who we would not use again because of feeling burned in the past. We've all been there. We've felt taken advantage of in some way when we've bought something, we've been told one thing and paid for something else, we've been let down along the way when our needs weren't met. These examples clearly illustrate the case of the seller getting his or her sale, not about having a satisfied customer as the end result.

No relationships are built in these cases, and we all have a tendency to share our misfortunes in our buying experiences with others. In fact, we can't wait to tell others. No company wants that to happen to them and to their valuable name. Most companies don't have a clear sense of what their sales staff are creating as a reputation with their precious company brand at risk.

Raising the profile of the salesperson to one of a trusted advocate is a clear way to increase sales for any business and remove the anticipated doubt and negative perceptions most consumers have of the world of sales. I hope to be able to share with you how you can do this. It's not rocket science and can make a world of difference in our challenging marketplace. Some simple changes can set you, personally, and whatever business you are in, apart from the crowd.

Create the relationship with your customers so that, like my grandchildren with the jalapeños, they are willing to try something new or different because they trust you. That relationship is the essence of *The Jalapeño Handshake.*

In the coming chapters, I'll address questions that may have occurred to you, such as:

- Why are some people and businesses successful while others aren't?

- What are the special elements that make up a trusting relationship?

- Why do I do things that I know I shouldn't do, or not do things I know I should?

- How do I feel good about what I do as a professional salesperson?

- Where do I even begin?

Because so many people—just like you—ask the same types of questions, answering these questions and others is the main goal of *The Jalapeño Handshake.*

Note: During the course of this book, I have commonly used the pronoun *he* when referring to an unspecified person. Obviously, in such instances the person can be either male or female. I tried to figure out an elegant way to include both sexes in my pronoun usage, but the clumsy *he or she* or even worse *s/he* were unacceptable. I finally gave up and used the tried-and-true, completely chauvinistic masculine pronoun. As a female, I was offended by my own grammatical crime against womanhood, but it's the best I could do. My apologies in advance if I have offended you as well.

# CHAPTER 1
## The Battle of Business

We don't need more strength or more ability or greater opportunity. What we need is to use what we have.

–Basil Walsh

# CHAPTER 1
## The Battle of Business

Read the business news these days, and you're almost guaranteed to see the headline, "Consumer Confidence Is Down." You need only look at the other headlines to figure out why. Banks are failing, insurance companies are failing, auto makers are failing, and respected businessmen with good reputations are discovered to have embezzled millions from their clients. It's almost as though every institution we thought we could depend on has let us down. Consumer confidence is down, and so is the confidence of many business owners.

There are promising signs of recovery in some areas of the business environment, and the economy is sure to bounce back as it always has. What has happened, however, is that customers and businesses have endured some harsh lessons and now approach financial decisions warily. Even in a recovering economy, the business environment can be tricky.

The marketplace today is more competitive than it has ever been. Big-box stores, supercenters, megastores, and superstores seem to pop up in every small town. Walmart is the 900-pound gorilla in the marketplace. According to *Fortune* magazine, in 2008, Walmart's sales were 50 percent higher than the next seven competitors—combined. In 1979, Walmart had fewer than 300 stores. In 2005, there were 3,800 stores in the United States and 2,800 more around the world.

One of the hardest times in a business owner's life is when a new Walmart opens nearby. Of course, it's not only one large company that's the challenge—every new large competitor that moves in divides the market and carries all the power and force of having a big name. Franchises and chain stores bring with them massive advertising budgets, and they have massive purchasing power, giving them the ability to undercut local businesses on price.

Along with the big-box stores, the entrepreneurial spirit seems to have erupted in recent years. More people are going into business for themselves, having become tired of working for other people and believing they have a chance to make a living—if not a fortune—as their own boss. Although a business owner can appreciate the dream of having a business competitor, he still has to battle for customers.

In almost any town of size, you will find an array of companies asking for your business. Specialty stores that cater to a particular niche in the market look for those people who want their product, and try to interest others in their specialty. Thirty years ago, no one would have ever considered paying more than 50 cents for a cup of coffee. Thanks to Starbucks, what was once a niche market—gourmet coffee—has become mainstream, and customers regularly pay several dollars for a cup.

Starbucks illustrates how a specialty store, when run correctly, can be very competitive in almost any market. The wide variety of choices and options open to consumers makes standing out more difficult. Consumers have become more sophisticated and know the subtleties of products.

Between the large international businesses and the tiny niche market specialty stores, the marketplace is more competitive than anyone could ever have dreamed. Only a few years ago, customers had far fewer choices. While running a business has never been easy, in recent times, attracting and retaining customers has become extremely difficult.

It's also more difficult to remain profitable. Rising costs force businesses to either raise their prices (and risk driving away hard-to-get customers) or eat the added expense and accept smaller profit margins. In a competitive retail environment, many customers are price conscious and base their purchasing decisions solely on price. A business can't afford to lose customers to the competition over the ill-advised philosophy, "profit above all."

At the same time, businesses have to have a margin if they are to keep their doors open. Business owners, therefore, are forced to find a delicate balance in pricing that lets them keep customers and still earn a profit. Unfortunately for many veteran business owners, that profit is much smaller than it used to be.

In a troubled economy, unemployment is high. When that's the case, customers don't have as much money to spend. A huge majority of businesses that offer non-essential products or services—non-essential, that is, to consumers who must choose between buying food and making the mortgage payment—compete fiercely for business, but there simply isn't enough money for customers to spend in all businesses.

Businesses may have problems making needed improvements because financial institutions have tightened their lending policies. What used to be a brief chat with a banker to get a loan has often become an examination by a committee to study your finances, your business plan, and your ability to repay.

For experienced businesspeople, the current business climate can be bewildering. Established consumer patterns have changed radically in the last few years. Technology has advanced business techniques in almost every conceivable way. Predicting what will happen in the marketplace from one day to the next is more difficult than ever.

Customers demand more from businesses, often more than a business is willing and able to provide. With the large number of options open to them, consumers know they can find what they want at the next business or the one after that. Today's business owner has to be smart, agile, and alert to what's going on around him.

To remain competitive, businesses must recognize the 24/7 access that consumers have to products. The choices are, if not infinite, practically so. The market has moved from a very slow selling process to a split-second one. The customer can often see a product on television, order it online, and have it delivered the next day, so building those trusting, deeper relationships with clients is ever more imperative. Businesses that can't keep up with this pace can be gone, metaphorically, in the space of a few mouse clicks.

Today's customer demands have created higher expectations than ever. With the vast quantity of available choices, customers can afford to ask for better and cheaper products and services, or any other option they perceive as valuable. In a competitive environment, consumers can almost always find what they want. They must simply find the store or service provider that wants their business enough to provide it.

Part of the challenge for businesses is that consumers have become more knowledgeable and sophisticated, thanks to the Internet. More information is available to the average person than at any time in history. Not only do consumers know all the add-ons, accessories, and extras that come with a product, but they can also find out how much other businesses are selling the product for. In other words, a local business is often competing with a business from across the country or even on the other side of the world.

Using the Internet, consumers know almost as much as or more about a product than the business owner. Although most businesspeople know their own products inside and out, they usually have many different products, and they also have the rest of their business to know. The consumer, on the other hand, has the luxury of being able to research one particular item in detail. When such a consumer walks into a store, the clerk may wind up learning about his own product.

With rising customer expectations, businesses have to demand more from their employees. To provide decent service, employees have to be more thoroughly trained. At a minimum, knowing all the basics is the price of admission to be able to serve in their product line. It's not enough to simply be able to run a cash register. For a business to compete, each employee must also be familiar with the company and its product line, and be able to answer any questions put to them. Businesses now have higher expectations of their employees as their brand and reputation representatives.

## TURNING "STRESSED" INTO "DESSERTS"

Annet, a personal account representative with Envision Financial, a large credit union located outside of Vancouver, British Columbia, exemplified great service when she set about easing some members' concerns about the recent market turmoil.

An elderly couple with over $1 million on deposit expressed to Annet their fear about the safety of their money. After all, they had seen firsthand the devastating effects of the Great Depression on their family farm. With the skill of a seasoned expert, Annet told them about the credit union's strength, its roots within the community, and the benefits of Credit Union Deposit Insurance Corporation (CUDIC) insurance. This, plus an account tweak to maximize insurance coverage, helped the members to once again feel confident about the safety of their Envision deposits.

The couple was so impressed with Annet's service that they invited her into their home for a feast befitting a queen, complete with china, crystal, and multiple courses to delight in. As they talked during the meal, the couple deepened their connection, laughing about life on the farm and at Annet's comedic stories of exploits as a young city girl being introduced to rural farming. The lunch ended with an array of desserts as a final thank-you to Annet for relieving their anxiety.

You can imagine how excited the couple was when a few weeks later Annet phoned them with the good news that 100 percent of their deposits were now insured. With a simple adjustment to their accounts, she was able to enhance the safety of their estate as well as their peace of mind.

》 Annet's story is a great example of advocating for the customer and providing the high level of service that customers yearn for when doing business with an organization. In fact, to truly advocate for a customer, an organization must be ready to think long-term and aim for results that are best for the customer, even if it means temporarily forsaking profit in return for goodwill. Let me give you an example from my banking days.

Interest-earning accounts are usually tiered based on their balance. That is, accounts with higher balances earn higher interest rates. An account with $15,000 would earn a higher interest rate than one with less than $5,000.

A customer might have two accounts, one with $10,000 and one with $5,000, each earning the lower interest rate. If the customer combined the two accounts, the larger balance would qualify for the higher interest rate. The bank obviously makes more profit from paying a lower interest rate. However, it is to the customer's benefit to combine the accounts and earn a higher interest rate (if they have no other reason for keeping the accounts separate). We instructed our associates to be advocates for the customer and to suggest just such a change when the need became apparent.

True, the bank would temporarily sacrifice the small profit it might realize on the difference in interest. But think about the huge amount of trust the bank earned when its employees approached customer relationships with this type of mindset. What the bank invests in the relationship it gains back tenfold in profit.

To maintain their market share, businesses have to provide more value to customers, simply to stay even. Business owners, then, not only expect more from their employees, but they also expect more from themselves. A successful business owner has a competitive streak and hates the idea that a competitor is taking away his customers by offering better value or service.

That competitive streak is what makes successful business owners dream of bigger things. They want not only to stay even but to gain more customers. They dream of building their business, opening several stores, franchising, and making a fortune. This kind of dream is what has always driven entrepreneurs to start businesses, and it's this dream that has made businesses remain competitive even in hard times.

The disappointment comes when all the work they do simply maintains the status quo, or worse, results in diminishing returns. The competition from all sides, the rising expenses, the problems with financing—these don't mean anything to a customer who is tightening his belt. When the economy is troubled, consumers shop where they perceive the best value, even though, thanks to manipulative advertising, the "deal" may unfortunately be only perception. So regardless of what the business owner does, the results of his efforts are often not enough to grow the business.

The result of all the hard work amounting to very little may be a profound sense of disappointment. Although a mature adult understands that disappointments are a part of life, no one is particularly happy when it happens. When you care about something deeply and have high hopes and expectations, falling short of those expectations often cuts deep.

Trying all they know to do, including techniques that have worked in the past, with results that are less than desired is very frustrating for the businessperson. That frustration comes from a feeling of helplessness, as though the business is no longer in his control. Experience is supposed to bring knowledge, but sometimes experience is not enough.

That frustration can easily turn to anger—anger at the economy, anger at the government, anger at the competition—even anger at the customer. The energy from anger is often what is required to move to a higher level of accomplishment, but it can often turn on the individual and become destructive. Uncontrolled anger damages everyone it touches.

With these negative emotions swirling around, the individual may easily fall into self-doubt. Instead of seeing the marketplace clearly, he becomes enmeshed in all the accompanying problems, criticizing every decision and judgment, and sometimes even becoming disillusioned with his career choice.

Why is it that traditional business techniques don't work? For one thing, the changing marketplace—the number of competitors, the higher customer expectations—means that there is a new set of rules for businesses. Unfortunately, no one seems to know what those rules are! What works one day doesn't work the next.

One of the reasons for the shifting rules is the plethora of information—some of it questionable—that is available to consumers. You never know when a new scientific study will make the headlines, putting a product or service at a disadvantage literally overnight.

During the late 1990s and into the early years of the twenty-first century, Krispy Kreme was the darling of investors. The doughnut shops opened everywhere, often causing lines around the block as patrons waited in line to get their Krispy Kreme.

At around the same time, scientific studies began to make headlines about the benefits of a "low-carb" diet. This diet advised people to avoid carbohydrates to lose weight. Although there were conflicting reports on the effects of such a diet on health, the low-carb diets became very popular.

One thing that doughnuts have in great supply is carbohydrates. As the popular media touted the benefits of cutting carbohydrates out of one's diet, Krispy Kreme doughnuts (always an obvious "naughty" food nutritionally) were suddenly on the bad list, the focus on carbs making them seem worse than ever, and sales began to drop.

The company's experience illustrates how difficult it is for even a well-run business to stay ahead of what happens in the marketplace. Practices and ideas that have proven themselves in previous years no longer work, and new strategies have to be implemented.

The companies that stay on top of the market and the industry become *buzzworthy*. "Buzz" occurs when people are talking about your company. Companies that deliver consistent service, superior products, and a high level of relationship with their customers create a buzz. Satisfied customers tell others about their experience. Adroit companies parlay these conversations into more business. They become worthy of the buzz, or buzzworthy.

The truth is that no single technique always works. Your business may have been built around the concept that "we do widgets better than anyone else." Although this slogan may still be true, in today's business environment, it's not enough. Customers realize that they have options, not only with different companies that produce widgets, but also in replacing widgets with something else entirely.

Occasionally a unique product or service comes along that cannot be replaced or reproduced. If that product or service becomes a necessity, then consumers will pay whatever price is necessary to obtain it. The business that provides such a product or service is in an enviable position.

Unfortunately, very few such items exist. Most products can be replaced with something else, duplicated, or reproduced more cheaply. Most services can be obtained more cheaply or more efficiently through some type of work-around. If a product or service is too expensive, consumers learn to do without it.

In such a business climate, how is your business supposed to survive and thrive? The first, most obvious point is that you have to know your business. Not only do you need to know your own company and how it works, but you must have a broader vision of your entire industry. You have to know your competition, including their strengths and weaknesses.

At the same time, you have to become aware of opportunities that might arise for your business. The first step in seeking opportunities is to listen to your existing customers. Do they ask for something that might complement what you offer? Is it something that you could provide?

Providing something different from what you previously have provided may mean that you must redefine your business. This doesn't mean that you suddenly switch from manufacturing carburetors to baking wedding cakes. It means going back to the first thought and using a broader vision of your industry to see what you're actually providing.

If you've ever been to a video rental store, you'll notice that they offer a variety of snacks—popcorn, candy, and other treats—as well as the standard movies. A large percentage of their profits comes from the sale of snack items to customers who come in to rent a movie. They started adding these items when they realized that they were not simply in the movie rental business, but were instead in the entertainment business. This broad redefinition of their business helped them provide more products to their customers.

A second point about competing in the current environment is that you have to look for, and accentuate, your company's advantages. They can be any number of things—the quality of your product or service, the price, its scarcity—the list is almost infinite. The question is whether the customer believes that your advantages are significant enough to do business with your company.

If your pizza parlor is the only one in town, it has a unique advantage in location. Your customers simply have to drive too far to get another pizza. However, if you price your pizza too high, your customers may choose to either do without or wait until they're in another area. In this case, you have pressed your advantage too far, and negative factors have overridden it.

This leads to a third point: that businesses have to focus on their long-term goals. Transacting business is simply another way of engaging in a relationship with your customers. If your goal is to stay in business for a long time, then it makes sense to treat your customers as you would anyone else with whom you want to have a long-term relationship.

The old-fashioned business philosophy of focusing solely on profits no longer works. That mindset results in the customer feeling "taken" when he conducts business. No relationship can last very long with that kind of imbalance. Both parties must feel as though they derive some benefit from dealing with the other.

Literally hundreds of thousands of products are offered in today's market. To repeat an earlier point, the Internet has brought the entire world into the homes of almost every computer user. It's very difficult to offer a unique product or always to have the lowest price. In this case, the competitive advantage is service.

## Differentiation

In business, the word *differentiation* is defined as the way in which your product or service stands out from the crowd. Although the concept of differentiation has been around for ages, in today's business environment, it's more important than ever. To obtain and keep a competitive advantage, a business must look for a way in which its customers can perceive that its product or service has more value than the competition's.

A business must do everything it can to retain its old customers. Simply trying to maintain the status quo, however, will eventually lead to decline. It's imperative that a company work to obtain new business. The goal with new business must be to acquire it, nurture it, and hang onto it. That can be done only by convincing customers of the advantages of your business's product or service. You have to offer more.

Differentiating between yourself and your competition is important in a number of ways. When you press your competitive advantage, customers perceive your product as better. For example, let's say that your company's product is better for the environment than your competitors'. If you do your job properly, when a competitor talks to one of your customers, the customer will ask, "How is your product for the environment?" You train your customers to believe in the superiority of your product.

You can't do this in a manipulative way, of course. Your product really must be better for the environment, as well as doing everything else it's supposed to do. By emphasizing your unique advantage, you increase the importance of that advantage to your customers.

When you provide a unique advantage, price loses some of its impact. Although all shoppers are looking for the best deal, if the advantage that differentiates you from everyone else in the marketplace is important enough to the customer, your product will be considered the best value, even if it's not the cheapest option.

Smart companies also differentiate themselves from their competition by selling solutions. Much is made of the busy lifestyles of families today. With no time to cook, they turn too often to low-nutrition fast food or low-quality frozen dinners. Crowded supermarkets make shopping for good food choices unpleasant and inefficient. How, then, can working parents provide nutritious, simple dinners for their families?

One Canadian company offered a solution to this dilemma. M&M Meat Shops offer nutritious, high-quality, reasonably priced heat-and-serve foods in their stores. Their options are menu-based, so customers can easily find what they need based on their dietary preferences. Because these dinner solutions are all they offer, the shops have a single aisle, and shoppers can find what they want quickly without the supermegamart hassle.

M&M Meat Shops separated itself from the competition by paying attention to their customers. They offered a unique solution to a problem that plagued many people. This type of thinking allows a company to flourish. With nearly 500 shops from coast to coast, M&M Meat Shops rank as Canada's largest chain of frozen-food stores.

One of the best features about differentiation is that it can be practiced at all levels of your organization. When you (or your receptionist) answer the phone, it can be as simple as saying, "Thank you for calling the XYZ Company, home of the million-dollar smile!" Delivery people can talk up your unique advantage. Customer service people can resolve issues efficiently, ending the call with, "Superior service is our goal."

Such differentiation applies to internal service as well. When a company can nail down outstanding service to each member at every level throughout its organization, the attitude absolutely overflows to the customers. *Attitude*, a much-used but often misunderstood word, is the combination of your thoughts, feelings, and actions. If every member of an organization has the right "wow" attitude, your company can perform service miracles.

Although these examples seem somewhat trite and simplistic, they illustrate how the concept of being different from the competition can permeate an organization. When everyone in the company thinks their organization has an advantage, you have the best advertising possible because the message is communicated to every customer. The unspoken message is, "When you think about (blank), think about our company."

This unique advantage that your company holds is known as the wow factor. It's a level of excellence that makes someone say "Wow!" when they first encounter it—a product of such high quality, or such a high level of service, that people are taken completely by surprise.

The wow factor should be something that customers can't get anywhere else. Note: The wow factor is not simply saying you're going to do or provide something for the customer—it's actually carrying through with your promise and delivering the goods. Customers have been inundated with promises via all the advertising they've endured over the years. What shocks them now is a company actually making good on the promise or being even better than promised.

Your customers will have an extraordinary perception of your business and will perceive your product or service at an entirely different level from that of your competitors. In some cases, your company, service, or product becomes synonymous with the industry that you're in. For example, those who want to record television programs speak of "TiVoing" the shows. TiVo holds such a special place in the market of digital video recording that its name has become a verb. It's the ideal product at the ideal time in today's culture.

The extra level of value that consumers crave is what you can provide. Using whatever you have that can uniquely impress your customers, you have the opportunity to lift your company above the competition to its own special place in their estimation.

The amazing thing about providing this wow experience to your customers is not that it will push you to such a lofty position that you no longer have to compete—it's that simply to stay viable, and to sustain your company's health and growth, you *have* to provide such an experience. If you don't do it, you can be sure that one of your competitors will.

## PARTNERSHIP BEFORE PROFIT

Several years ago, when I was Vice President of Sales and Service for Vancity Credit Union, I had a great opportunity to see a top-level example of a company that put its belief in relationships into action.

As an added service, Vancity gave its members/customers the opportunity to purchase creditor insurance. If the customer became unable to make payments on a loan due to temporary disability, the loan payments would be paid by the insurance until the customer was able to resume payment. If the customer were to die, the loan would be paid off completely. The actual insurance was provided by another company; Vancity merely made it available via its branches and through its employees.

Vancity, in the process of making changes to its insurance offerings, decided to do business with CUMIS, an insurance services company. Vancity is a huge organization, and the changeover in insurance providers necessitated a completely new system, with new reports, new paperwork, and new computer programs. Every Vancity employee involved—hundreds of them—would have to be trained in the new system. CUMIS, eager to establish a good relationship with Vancity, worked extremely hard to ensure that Vancity employees received the training they needed to confidently and easily offer CUMIS's suite of insurance products.

Because of the lengths CUMIS went to, the transition went smoothly, and Vancity and CUMIS have formed a productive relationship. If the story were to end there, it would be a good story—but there's more. As the relationship between CUMIS and Vancity matured, CUMIS began to find new and imaginative ways to form a strategic partnership with Vancity, identifying ways they could help Vancity reach its long-term goals. There was no mention of how CUMIS would profit—the only concern expressed was how they could strengthen their credibility and trustworthiness with Vancity so that the two organizations could create a stronger relationship.

When Vancity originally chose CUMIS to provide insurance to its members, it risked its credibility and good reputation with those members, as well as with its own employees. Bad service and/or bad products would have been disastrous for the credit union. What they found in CUMIS, however, was a partner who earned their trust, and they became true partners.

## )) Value proposition

To define the particular way in which they can provide value to their customers, some companies create a *value proposition*. A value proposition is simply a short statement that states the tangible results a customer gets when using your product or services. It could be called an "elevator speech" or a "back of the napkin" presentation, or any number of names, but the idea is the same—it defines your company's value to the customer.

M&M Meat Shops provide a great example of a value proposition. The founders started the company with a clear idea of what they offered. They wanted to create a place where people could purchase choice cuts of restaurant-quality meat and specialty food items at reasonable prices. This powerful value proposition doubtlessly has contributed to the company's success.

When you create a value proposition, it's important that you keep your focus on the customer. This statement is about tangible benefits your customers receive. It could be about saving money, greater reliability, ease of use, peace of mind—whatever it is you can provide that your competition cannot.

Obviously, if you have created the perception in the customer's mind that he will benefit from doing business with you, your company will benefit also. Such a perception will separate you from, and elevate you over, your competition. When a person believes that he has found a great bargain, he can't wait to tell others about it. What this means is that salespeople get more and better leads because of these referrals.

## Salespeople

Because they have more contact with customers than anyone else in the company, salespeople hold a special place in helping your company position itself in the customer's mind. Salespeople are the ones who match the customer's needs with the appropriate product or service that your company provides. The ability to make that match well is crucial in the business cycle.

Without salespeople, customers would not have all the information they need to make a good decision. Even with the vast quantity of information available to them, customers still need someone to help match their particular needs with the product that best meets those needs. That takes someone with knowledge of both the product (with all its subtleties and special features) and the customer's specific requirements. The salesperson is the only one who provides that knowledge.

A good salesperson is also a problem solver. Life is not always smooth, and occasionally the salesperson is in a position to help a customer in need. They might need a product right away or a particular service sooner than normally scheduled. The salesperson is your company's representative on the spot, able to provide a solution.

This aspect of the salesperson's position is often overlooked. Salespeople are the eyes and ears of their company. They see conditions in the real world—what the competition is doing, where construction is going on—any number of conditions that can affect the company.

Besides external conditions, the salesperson knows what's on the mind of his customers. A single customer might make an unusual request for some passing, arbitrary reason. If several customers make similar requests, however, a situation has developed that only the salesperson is in a position to recognize.

)) One aspect of salespeople that is often overlooked is that they are the only people who generate revenue. Without the salespeople talking to customers and bringing in orders, none of the rest of the company could function. Shortsighted executives sometimes forget this fact and cut salespeople when times are hard. Eventually, they cut themselves so short that their diminishing revenue stream forces them out of business.

## Sales as a dirty word

Despite all the benefits I have listed, many salespeople view *sales* as a dirty word, something to be ashamed of. They have allowed themselves to be influenced by the media stereotype of the pushy, rude, in-your-face salesman. The stereotypical salesman from movies and television is always fast-talking and as likely to lie to you as not. He is in it only for the money, doing whatever he needs to do to make a buck.

That's silly, of course. We are sophisticated and mature enough to recognize other stereotypes from the movies and to discard them. Every human being is an individual, and the vast majority of professional salespeople are honest, caring, and as courteous as your mother.

In fact, the average salesperson might *be* your mother or someone else's mother. They are the same people you associate with every day. Their profession doesn't change that. In fact, the true professionals use honesty and caring as part of their profession. They recognize that they are in a relationship and that treating other people well is the most profitable route in the long term.

We are all salespeople in one way or another. When we try to convince someone of the superiority of a particular view or idea, we are selling the benefits of that view or idea. One of the best salespeople in the world is the toddler who wants something. Merely by pointing and grunting, he knows that Mommy will get it for him. If she doesn't, he convinces her by crying.

This means that the entire world's population is made up of salespeople. Most are amateurs, using sales techniques—emphasizing the advantages of their idea, point of view, or plan—to meet the needs and to influence the decisions of other people. Others are professionals, who use those same techniques to earn a living.

I'm not recommending that you cry to convince your customers, but it's important that you look at sales as an honorable profession providing a vital service. Think of the fundraisers for charities that help millions of people around the world. Each of those fundraisers is a salesperson, reaching out to contributors to help.

The best salespeople build long-term relationships with their customers. They understand that they can't do that if they are seeking to take advantage of the other person. By always ensuring a win-win transaction—one in which both parties have benefited—salespeople at all levels continue the tradition of meeting the needs of their customers.

# CHAPTER 2
## Your Personal Prison

No one can go back and make
a brand new start. Anyone can
start from now and make a
brand new ending.

–Unknown

# CHAPTER 2
## YOUR PERSONAL PRISON

Our work lives, as well as our personal lives, should be exciting and rewarding, yet many of us meekly endure each day, dreading tomorrow. The negative emotions that hold many salespeople back, and that many people in all fields of business share, have the same roots as the emotions and attitudes that hold us back in all aspects of our personal lives.

As individuals, we often don't make the best choices in life. Sometimes we refuse to make a choice, which in itself is a choice. It has become a cliché in movies to show what happens to the young man at the prom who wants to dance with the beautiful girl yet lacks the courage to ask her. Other examples all feel familiar: the employee who didn't apply for a promotion, the student who never tried out for the team, the salesperson who passed up a lead.

These examples demonstrate a *lack of confidence*. A lack of confidence may be caused by a number of issues. You may not feel worthy enough as a person. You may feel as though you will humiliate yourself if you try something new. You may have tried something once and had a bad experience. In any case, confidence—belief in yourself and in your abilities—is not present, at least not in sufficient quantities to enable you to take action.

Another mindset that may be holding you back is apathy, or a *lack of passion*. If you respond "Whatever" when someone asks your opinion, don't have any real hobbies or interests (sorry, watching television doesn't count), and can't readily think of a goal that you'd like to accomplish, then passion is definitely missing.

Why is passion important? Because the road to success in any endeavor is rough, and only passion can help you through hard times. Perseverance stems from passion, a vision of the future that is better than your present. Passion ignites the hard work involved in carrying out a mission to its successful conclusion.

Many cultures are passionate by nature—individuals are willing to engage other people to get what they want—while other cultures have developed the idea that showing passion is unnatural or impolite. Some families exhibit their passion at the dinner table, with loud discussion, emotion, and drama a part of every meal. Contrast them with those families whose meals are always quiet, polite, and distant. Your cultural upbringing can determine how much passion you bring to bear on a task or project.

Another trait that can hold you back is complacency, or *lack of drive*. Complacency is marked by the willingness to settle for what you've got, even when you know that—with a little effort—you could improve your life. Like passion and confidence, your sense of drive may have been conditioned out of you.

In some circles, striving for success is actually discouraged. Family or friends who have already given up on life actively chastise and ridicule those who work to improve themselves. Enough of that kind of treatment can take the wind out of your sails completely. For people who have been victims of such a mentality from those close to them, success has come to equal pain. They live by the pessimistic credo, "Better to simply sit quietly and take what life gives you."

In today's world, it's common to find people who *lack the physical energy* to improve their lives. Amidst an abundance of food, we are undernourished. With all of the luxuries of modern society, we are physically unfit and unhealthy. With all of the food additives, chemicals, and modern distractions we encounter, our sleep is interrupted to the extent that we are always tired.

Is it any wonder then that a group of people who are unhealthy and exhausted have trouble finding the energy to climb the ladder of success? I'm sure you know of people who seem to have boundless energy and are always working on another project. They are the ones who have found a way to take care of their primary tool—their physical body—and who know how to periodically recharge their batteries.

The last trait that can hold people back—and somewhat surprisingly, the least common—is a *lack of skills*. Learning the skills to be successful is an external exercise that everyone can take advantage of. However, if those other, internal traits have not been addressed, then developing your skills won't help. Conversely, when you conquer the conditions that have held you back, developing skills becomes less important and, when they are necessary, they are more easily mastered.

Considering the negative influences surrounding us, no wonder many of us have negative feelings about our jobs. Society seems to thrive on negativity. The headlines are bad news, problems seem to reverberate to an insurmountable point, and everyone seems to have a grudge against someone else. Although we strive hard to eliminate our prejudices and biases, entire classes of people are judged solely on the kind of work they do.

A while back I read a poll that determined which professions were the least trusted. Not surprisingly, politician and used-car salesman were considered the least trustworthy. Heavy media saturation of stereotypes portrayed in movies and on television strongly influences the public's perception. Otherwise enlightened people make judgments based on stories that are created to entertain.

Unfortunately, we are surrounded by those same people. Our family members often hold the same negative perception of a profession. When you are raised in such an environment, it takes a revelation from an outside source to enable you to reach a different conclusion. If you have negative feelings about your job, it may be due to your family's influence.

The media have influenced our perception of business and salespeople, almost never in a positive way. From the unfortunate Willy Loman in *Death of a Salesman* to *Boiler Room* to the cult comedy *Office Space*, those characters engaged in business are often portrayed as either weak, greedy, unscrupulous, or a combination of those traits.

Salespeople in particular suffer from stereotypical treatment in movies and television. The truth is that salespeople are not a separate species, existing simply to leech off their customers. Although no doubt there are unscrupulous salespeople, it is a mistake to judge the sales profession or those who practice it by the fictional characters we see on screen. Unfortunately, such images are powerful and hold great influence over us—unless we are aware of their influence and fight it.

A more unfortunate negative influence on how we feel about our jobs is that of those people who, disillusioned and discouraged, have given in to negativity. They have years of experience in their job and may be called veterans, old-timers, or simply more experienced. They may have achieved marginal success by compromising their principles and sacrificing their ethics, until they believe that doing so is the only way to get by in business. It should go without saying that there are not many shortcuts on the road to success. Those who concentrate on cutting corners will rarely achieve lasting success.

Those who have chosen to work in this way seem also to be the most vocal about how business works. As veterans of business, they ought to have credibility. You may find yourself listening to them and even believing them. After all, if they've been at it for this long, they must know *something*, right?

The answer to that question is, no, of course not. Cheaters never truly win, and their attitude may be the source of negative emotions you have toward your job. If you constantly hear that you must compromise your principles in order to do your work, how can you possibly feel good about it? As hard as it is, give credence only to advice that rings true. Doing the right thing is almost always more difficult than cheating, but in the long run it is much more rewarding.

If you have negative feelings toward your job and the work you do, you instantly place limitations on yourself. You will wear blinders that restrict your future possibilities. If you see the future at all, it will be in a negative, depressing way. The persistent question in the back of your mind will be "What's the use?" Such an attitude will automatically restrict the amount of enthusiasm with which you approach each day's tasks.

If you are in sales with a negative attitude about your profession, then the word *no* will become a tremendous setback every time you hear it, rather than simply another part of the sales process. The most successful salespeople greet the word *no* with gusto, because they see it as the customer's way of asking for more information. The least successful salespeople take *no* as a defeat and move on to the next transaction.

With a negative attitude about your work, you will ultimately settle for less, placing one of the most harmful limitations on yourself. It means that you have given up trying, so the promotion, the raise, the rewards go to someone else. This, of course, fits in with and reinforces the negative belief system that you've constructed. You see the world through mud-colored glasses.

Sometimes the restrictions you put on your own success have to do with the perception you have not only of yourself but also of "people like you." You may come from a small town or lack the level of formal education that you think you should have. Your family may have lived with limited financial resources. Regardless of the reason, when you judge yourself as a class of person, rather than as an individual, you take away the potential that exists in each of us.

We retain these mistaken and unuseful belief systems because, on a very fundamental level, they work. They satisfy some value that we hold, perhaps subconsciously. For example, a salesman might subconsciously sabotage his sales because he earns more money than his father ever earned. Most people love their parents and would never do anything to hurt them. The salesman might believe that his greater success will somehow hurt his father's feelings.

Valid or not, such a belief has power. In this example, that belief helped the salesman avoid the pain of causing pain to his father. In a twisted sense, it worked. Most of us hold beliefs that would not stand up to scrutiny if we were conscious of them and examined them rationally. Without such examination, however, these beliefs continue to hold power over us.

We also hold on to mistaken beliefs because we are comfortable with them. Examining your beliefs takes courage, and changing them takes energy. We hold certain patterns of thought because routine helps us get through the day. We constantly make decisions without thought, because it would be impossible to get through a day—even an average day, an easy day— if we had to stop everything and figure out a solution for each decision we make.

Think about it. Your alarm goes off in the morning, and you have to decide whether to get up right away or hit the snooze button. Should you brush your teeth first or shower? What's for breakfast—eggs, cereal, juice, a protein shake? Should you wear your jacket or carry it with you? Read the morning paper now or save it for later? Dozens of decisions must be made, and you haven't even set foot out the front door!

We establish habits based on our belief systems. You may have put effort into the decision at one time—you save time by avoiding the snooze button, for example—but once the decision is made, you live with it. Only an outside influence can force you to reinspect your habits and beliefs to determine whether they still work. Without the possibility of greater rewards (or less pain) to help you change, you automatically stick with the most comfortable routine.

Another reason we adhere to mistaken beliefs is because our current lifestyle, unhappy and unproductive as it may be, provides our sense of identity. This belief is related to the "people like us" syndrome, in which your identity is based on your socioeconomic class, your race, your geographic location, or some other factor. The thought goes something like this: *People like us don't earn a lot of money.* Or, *People like us aren't cut out to be leaders.*

Your sense of identity is a powerful yet, at the same time, very fragile force. It controls many of the decisions you make in your life and affects how you feel about a given situation. If you make changes in your life that threaten your sense of identity, you feel discomfort. Only when you have a powerful motivator that helps you work through the discomfort are you able to make changes to improve your life.

Along the same lines, pressure from those around you can force you to adhere to mistaken beliefs. There are always kids in school who have the ability to make good grades yet hold themselves back because they want to remain within their social circle—they want to belong. Doing well on tests and working to achieve success in school places them in the "brains" category, and their friends ridicule them for their efforts. Eventually, many students simply quit trying and accept their place within the group.

Ultimately, all of these pressures result in *programming*. Programming is simply the way your mind works. It's a set of impressions that have been imprinted on your brain since birth, determining your beliefs, your values, and all the decisions that stem from them. Through repetition over time, your programming becomes a well-traveled mental road. Without your even being aware of it, programming influences how you will react when you encounter a new situation.

Because of your programming, when you make a decision, you automatically eliminate certain options, while giving more consideration to others. This happens so quickly and so subtly that you don't even realize you're doing it. That's why brainstorming exercises with others work so well. If your goal is simply to create the greatest number of solutions instead of worrying about their quality, your natural inhibitions (created by your programming) don't have a chance to kick in.

Besides your decisions, your programming also affects your dreams and vision for the future. Certain futures simply don't come to mind because they are contrary to your programming. Healthy individuals with open minds have more options simply because their programming allows it. Those people who have been programmed with many restrictions have fewer options because they can't see alternatives.

## ))) Overcoming faulty programming

The thinking pattern that restricts your possibilities is called *faulty programming*. If we agree that one definition of success is to have more options rather than fewer options, then you can see how overcoming faulty programming is vital to living a richer, more fulfilling life. How then, do you go about breaking unuseful thought patterns?

As with any obstacle that you're trying to overcome, the first step is to recognize that it exists. Everyone has programming of one kind or another. High achievers are those individuals who realize they have weaknesses and work hard to minimize them. Look at the decisions you make and the process you use to reach them, and see if there are times when you are blind to certain options. Examine your language and see if you use hyperbolic words such as *never* and *always*. These may indicate that unconscious biases guide you.

If you find that your programming affects your decisions, examine it and see whether it's useful. The term *usefulness* describes any activity or mental process that moves you closer to your goals. You may find that some of your programming is very useful indeed—for example, feeling confident is necessary when calling on new customers. If you discover that a particular aspect of your programming is a source of strength for you, keep it. If it's not, decide whether you need to change it.

Changing your programming can occur only after you have acknowledged and evaluated it. Identifying aspects of your programming—your beliefs, biases, and inclinations—will help you pick and choose so that you keep the parts that work and eliminate those parts that don't.

Changing your programming requires that you replace it with something else. There are many ways to accomplish this. You can use affirmations, read inspirational literature, study successful people, seek out mentors— the list of possibilities is long. The main goal is to saturate yourself with positive messages to support your new program until it is strong enough to carry itself. Otherwise, the old programming will reassert itself, and you will revert back to the old mindset.

For example, you might feel trepidation about earning above a certain amount. Trying to imagine yourself earning over $100,000 a year, for example, may seem completely unrealistic and impossible ("for someone like you"—at least, that's what your mind tells you). You can repeat affirmations to yourself each morning, something simple, such as, "I enjoy earning my $100,000 and put it to good use." (Or, as I recently heard, "The secret to success is having a healthy disregard for the impossible.")

You might begin reading rags-to-riches stories, revealing how others have moved to a higher level of success. Read books about how to become more successful in all areas of your life. Joining an organization in which you have the opportunity to associate with others who have achieved success or who are working toward their success is another option.

Consider joining or creating a Master Mind group. Napoleon Hill, the author of *Think and Grow Rich*, defined a Master Mind group as "a coordination of knowledge and effort, in the spirit of harmony, between two or more people, for the attainment of a definite purpose." Reading books, listening to tapes, associating with other like-minded individuals—all of these activities reinforce the idea that it's possible for *you* to be successful and to earn as much money as you want.

To further reinforce your new programming, think also of why your new mindset is important. For example, you might envision being able to provide better for your family, or your children going to a better college. In other words, the programming you add should have more value than the end result (as in the $100,000 example above). It's often been said that the *why* of achieving success is more important than the *how*.

I've had my own experiences in which my old programming, my internal voice, has prevented me from moving in the direction of my dreams. While some experiences were less important in the grand scheme of things, one in particular resulted in my losing a very precious gift, the gift of trust. I certainly didn't realize it at the time, but after much analysis and reflection, I came to understand some of what had prevented me from taking different action. The other person and I each had our own faulty programming, and our wires crossing left a very deep hole. It was a tough lesson to learn but one that taught me never to allow old programming to dictate my choices.

When you are replacing old programming, try to remember that implementing changes can often be scary. You are reconstructing your sense of identity. With this in mind, try to find ideas and concepts that excite you a lot and scare you only a little. If the idea of earning $100,000 a year doesn't excite you, find the dollar amount that does. If earning a million dollars a year scares you too much, drop the amount until it's at a level you can handle. By approaching your changes in such a way—and constantly reevaluating your new programming to check its effectiveness—you will begin to move your mind closer to your goals.

## )) Your own worst enemy

Old programming is part of the explanation for a phenomenon that many of us suffer from—self-sabotage. You may have seen it in other people or even suffered from it yourself. An opportunity presents itself, something that is very desirable to you. You begin to work toward it but then inexplicably do something that defeats your own purpose. You have become your own worst enemy.

Such behavior is often caused by the force of old programming. You realize that you want something, yet old habits, biases, prejudices, or ways of thinking run counter to your new goal. Subconsciously, achieving the new goal is painful to old programming, and those forces push you into self-destruction.

The fear of change also can lead you to sabotage your own progress. Your comfort level, sense of identity, and anxiety about losing the approval of your peers all contribute to that fear. You are working with contradictory motivations—on one hand, you want to improve your life and situation, and on the other, you want your life to stay the same. Often the pressures for the latter win out, and you wind up collapsing while working toward a goal.

Oddly, the fear of success can sometimes cause you to sabotage yourself. You may have worked hard on a project to ensure its success, only to fall short at a crucial point. Perhaps you've started a project with great enthusiasm, but as the project nears completion, you become less enthusiastic. Both of these circumstances can be symptoms of a fear of success.

Whenever we work toward something that we've never done before, we may feel as though we're performing "over our head"—in other words, actually performing better than we're capable of. In our minds, there will be pressure to maintain that level of performance. When we fail to sustain it, others will know that we're impostors and that our earlier success was a fluke.

If that argument rings any bells with you, realize that you're not alone. Even famously successful people are often afraid of being "found out," that other people will discover that they're not as talented, as intelligent, or as gifted as everyone assumes. What these success stories have done, however, is to continue to work toward their goals. No one is successful one hundred percent of the time. Think of all the big Hollywood actors who have starred in the most successful movies. Each one of those stars has been in several less-than-successful movies. However, they continued to act and to work for their dreams.

We can also sabotage ourselves if we try to work without a plan. Many people feel that if they bustle around enough, creating activity, they will be successful. Of course, occasionally someone will have momentary success through sheer energy, but that is the rare occurrence.

More often, through careful thought and execution of a plan, individuals achieve success. For some, this is uncomfortable. They are doers, not thinkers. While energy is good, and even necessary, it takes a combination of brain effort and body effort to be successful consistently.

Self-sabotage often manifests itself emotionally. You may feel apathy about achieving your goals or even hostility about achieving something that should be of benefit to you. Your energy levels may become extremely low as a result of your inner conflict. Exhaustion and even depression can settle on you as your old programming tries to exert its influence against your new mindset.

Self-sabotage is always the manifestation of your old programming. It may not have an external cause at all. However, if you've ever found yourself settling for less, never wanting more, then you could be in self-sabotage mode. Your lack of self-assertion, or even outright laziness, is old programming doing everything it can to prevent you from making the most of your life.

Self-sabotage creates tough situations for anyone who suffers from it, but for salespeople, it can be disastrous. The shame some salespeople feel about their profession is one of the ways that old programming causes destruction. If you're ashamed of what you do, it's pretty difficult to be successful at it.

More common is the salesperson's easy acceptance of the word *no*. Any salesperson with more than an hour's worth of experience has run into a customer who has said no. It's a normal part of the sales process. However, successful salespeople understand that a customer's instinctive response to an offer is *always* to say no. Only through further communication will the average customer make the deal. Accepting *no* too quickly and easily makes for a tough career in sales.

A related aspect of self-sabotage is the reluctance to cold-call. Cold-calling is simply the presentation of your product or service to someone who has not yet seen it. Salespeople often make a huge obstacle out of this process, creating an unpleasant and unnerving experience. Yet only by getting new customers can a sales professional thrive in the business. If you've worked cold-calling into a massive mountain that you can't climb, you are sabotaging your own progress.

Similarly, timidity or defensiveness in presenting your product can only slow you down. One of the tenets of the ethical salesperson is that you must feel good about what you are selling. Of course, no product is perfect, but if your product or service's soft spots are what you are focused on, you will quickly begin to have negative feelings about the product. Focus on the positive attributes of what you are selling so that you can present it confidently to customers.

## Doing what's been done

Albert Einstein is rumored to have said, "The definition of insanity is doing the same thing over and over again, and expecting different results." Unless you are achieving wild success in your business, doing the same old thing in today's demanding business environment will only hold you back. Adaptability is the new watchword. Only by looking for new ways to achieve success will you be able to compete.

Unless you have managed to differentiate yourself from your competitors and have communicated that uniqueness to your customers, you are doomed to eventual failure. You will fall behind those who have learned to adapt.

Businesses are susceptible to old programming, just as individuals are. They may rely on conventional wisdom as an excuse for their lack of innovation or flexibility. Business programming comes from some of the same sources as our individual programming—family, peers (usually in the form of former bosses or co-workers), and schools. Many of these influences come with the title of *expert* attached—a title that carries more weight than it sometimes should.

One expert in his field was Charles Duell, Commissioner of the U.S. Patent Office. In 1899, he issued his most famous opinion: "Everything that can be invented has been invented." Fortunately for those of us who enjoy such luxuries as television, computers, and air conditioning, Mr. Duell was mistaken.

Old business programming often carries the same attitude as Mr. Duell, with the same lack of accuracy. Overcoming that programming means recognizing that the world changes with every passing moment. We either embrace change, reset our measurements, and look to innovate and redefine the value that we offer, or we get left behind.

Being willing to innovate also means looking for new challenges, because with every new challenge comes a new opportunity.

# CHAPTER 3
## Playing Well with Others

WHEN YOU DANCE, YOUR PURPOSE IS
NOT TO GET TO A CERTAIN PLACE ON
THE FLOOR. IT'S TO ENJOY EACH STEP
ALONG THE WAY.

–Dr Wayne Dyer

# CHAPTER 3
## Playing Well with Others

The English poet and philosopher John Donne wrote, "No man is an island, entire of itself." Each of our interactions with another person connects and ripples across multiple lives. Every conversation and every action affects that one person and that person's impression of us. They, in turn, interact with other people in a way that reflects that impression.

Realizing the tremendous impact you have on other people, and the impact they have on you and everything you do, puts the importance of maintaining healthy relationships into perspective. If you blunder through your interactions with others without thought of the consequences, you will often do as much harm as good. By the same token, working diligently and purposefully to establish positive relationships can be the key to creating a successful life.

When it comes to relationships, most people first think of their family. Some people enjoy close, supportive relationships with their parents, their brothers and sisters, their children, and their extended family, including aunts, uncles, cousins, and grandparents. They have learned early in life the benefit of these relationships and developed the skills necessary to be part of such relationships.

Others, for various reasons, may not enjoy such happy relationships. Broken families, single-parent (or even no-parent) families, and dysfunctional families unfortunately are common. Even when a family is intact, distance and coolness between family members may prevent the development of close bonds.

Friendships also develop along a spectrum of intimacy and bonding, from very close friends you can count on to "have your back" to poisonous friends who drag you down. Friendships sometimes are created in situations in which an individual's characteristics are desirable, but once outside that particular situation, the same trait becomes a liability. An irresponsible, fun-loving friend you enjoyed partying with in high school or college may not be compatible with your lifestyle once you are married and supporting a family.

Most of us have a large network of acquaintances with whom we come in contact regularly, but who are not close enough to be considered friends. The person who cuts your hair, the supermarket checker, your mail carrier, your dry cleaner—you depend on all of these people for their contributions to your well-being. You're not close enough to share all the details of your life story with them, but you rub up against them enough that your interactions are significant.

Your co-workers may fit into both categories. Some of the people with whom you work may be your friends, whereas others are little more than acquaintances. Co-workers are significant in that we often spend more time with them than we do our own families. Regardless of our profession, most of us try to project a professional image when dealing with co-workers. With a few we share parts of our lives, and the information we share may or may not complement the image we present to the rest of the company.

As a member of a business, either as employer or employee, you likely have some dealings with customers, even if only occasionally. These interactions reflect not only on you personally but also on your business. If you are cold, aloof, and unhelpful with a customer, he or she will likely form the same impression of your company.

If you are in sales, your job requires you to have extensive interactions with customers. Every professional salesperson knows that customer relationships can make or break his paycheck. An effective salesperson can't afford to be haphazard in relationships with customers. Those interactions are the very essence of the salesperson's job.

Finally, the interactions we have with strangers can affect our lives tremendously. If you are driving to work and another car cuts you off, do you respond calmly or do you go directly to road rage? Does that anger carry over into your workplace? Such casual, one-time interactions with strangers can cause us to do or say things that we normally would avoid.

On the other hand, have you ever been touched emotionally when a stranger opened a door for you or helped you pick up items you dropped? The movie *Pay It Forward* portrays this theme dramatically. As part of a school project to "change the world," a young boy helps a stranger, with the admonition to "pay it forward." The entire movie shows the cumulative effect of people helping one another, for no other reason than to extend a hand. Such interactions can change lives.

These interactions with others, whether with family, friends, or strangers, are what establish the value of your life. If relationships and interacting with other people are of low value to you, and you avoid them, your whole life will be like a stone thrown into a pond—the ripples will last for just a few minutes, and then it will be as though you had never been there.

On the other hand, if you value other people and treat them with respect and honesty, your life will be well spent. Not only the quality of your time on earth, but also the example and lessons you provide during your lifetime will positively affect hundreds, if not thousands, of people.

With all this talk of relationships, it's time for you to evaluate your relationships. For busy people—and who's *not* busy these days?—it's difficult to maintain good relationships at the level they deserve. Only by renewing and refocusing your relationships can you be sure that you are making maximum contributions to the quality of your life.

Work on shoring up those relationships you think could be stronger. Look at them objectively to determine whether there is tension or distance that you hadn't noticed before. (A large part of maintaining a good relationship is noticing.) Sometimes an undercurrent of tension can be resolved by simply asking the other person, "Is everything okay between us? There seems to be some tension, and I'd like to resolve it, because I value our relationship."

These conversations can be difficult. There's always the chance that you will hear about something you did wrong. Being this forthright can be hard, because not everyone is eager to discuss their feelings. However, with this simple approach, you've done several things:

- You've acknowledged that you pay attention to the quality of the relationship and notice when it has deteriorated.

- You've confirmed to the other person that you value them and that you want to remove the obstacle that has sprung up between you.

- You've given the other person the opening to discuss what they perceive to be the problem.

This approach won't work immediately in every difficult circumstance, but it's the first step toward creating the dialogue that must take place to heal a wounded relationship. Very often, you will have to read the other person's feelings to determine if you need to give them emotional breathing room. Some people are so terrified of confrontation that they will avoid telling you anything unpleasant, even if it might improve the relationship. Be alert to such emotions and give the other person the support they need to help mend the problem between you.

On the other end of the spectrum are the relationships that you feel are strongest. These are likely the friends and family with whom you share values and who are in constant communication with you. These are the people you can count on in times of trouble, and who can count on you. Your goal is to make these relationships even stronger.

How do you go about doing that? In his book *The 7 Habits of Highly Effective People*, Stephen R. Covey discusses the concept of the "emotional bank account." As with a regular bank account, you make deposits and withdrawals, except instead of money, you use emotions. When you help a friend move furniture, you are making a deposit. When you make time to have a conversation with your daughter about something that's important to her, you make a deposit.

Even with the strongest relationships, you can get your emotional bank account into the red. If you ask a friend for a favor too many times, no matter how good the friendship is, he will eventually begin to feel that you are taking advantage of him. Go to a friend complaining about your life too many times, and he will begin to avoid having conversations with you. You are making too many withdrawals from the emotional bank account, and your account is overdrawn.

To strengthen already-strong relationships, focus on making deposits into your emotional bank account. Show kindnesses, both large and small, without being asked. Volunteer to help whenever you can. If you are asked why you are being so thoughtful, tell them simply, "I value our relationship, and I want to make sure that you know it."

Of course, this technique is also useful with relationships that may have deteriorated. However, if you start doing favors for someone when your relationship is on rocky ground, they may suspect you of ulterior motives or of being manipulative. In that case, what you consider deposits, the other person considers withdrawals. Trust must be established before deposits into the emotional bank account can be made.

Finally, look at establishing new relationships. Perhaps you have acquaintances you'd like to know better. Bear in mind that they likely classify you in the same way, so sudden aggressiveness on your part may surprise them. But if you already engage them in conversation, ask questions to find out their interests and concerns. Becoming genuinely interested in other people is the key to forming new relationships. Always keep in mind the concept of making deposits into the emotional bank account. Deposits count only if they are of value to the other person, and you can know that only if you genuinely care about them.

## Creating relationships

Of course, I don't mean randomly talking to strangers in hopes of creating new relationships. Although such an approach would certainly create an interesting life, it would also waste a lot of time, in addition to alarming strangers wary of your sudden interest in them! What you are looking for is *productive* relationships.

What is a productive relationship? It's one in which both parties profit. For example, you would never approach someone to invest in your company if he were not going to earn a profit. You would merely be using that person for funding. However, if you offer a potential investor a solid chance at a good return on his money, you both would benefit from the relationship. It would be productive.

In the movie *Groundhog Day* (by now you may have figured out that I am a movie buff), Bill Murray's character relives the events of a single day over and over. In one scene he runs into an old classmate he has not seen in years. The classmate now sells insurance, and after a perfunctory greeting, begins trying to sell Murray an insurance policy. Needless to say, Murray cannot get rid of the guy fast enough. He had struck up a conversation only to make a sale.

If you approach a new relationship with only your own goals in mind, it is doomed to fail. A productive relationship requires balance to survive and thrive. Of course, you have objectives that you want to achieve, but they cannot be your primary motivation. Benefits to the other person have to be established early on, in order for a relationship to take hold.

In a productive relationship, the interests of both parties are advanced. In the example of the potential business partner mentioned before, the financial well-being of each party was advanced. For others, emotional well-being might be improved. For that to happen, you must be able to foster positive emotions. The other person in turn fosters your emotional well-being. In a productive relationship, financial or emotional, your interaction is win-win. Everyone benefits.

Such relationships are much more fulfilling when you share core values, such as honesty, trust, respect, and communication. When you share values, you hold similar outlooks on life. The bonds that connect you are strong.

You do not have to agree with the other person's every opinion, however. People of integrity can hold different beliefs on any topic, even such hot button issues as politics or religion. When you share core values, those differences can be discussed without threatening the relationship. Differences can be acknowledged and respected.

In a fulfilling, productive relationship, the relationship itself takes primary importance. Differences can be discussed without either person feeling diminished or threatened, as long as both parties respect each other. Holding the individual in high regard is a key requirement for a strong relationship. When you have that kind of regard for someone, personal attacks are not even a consideration. The relationship takes priority.

When you have established boundaries you both respect, a relationship of this kind recharges and revitalizes you. When you agree on something, you feel better, and both your interests are advanced. When you disagree— agreeably—you are presented with a different viewpoint that may open your own mind to new possibilities. You advance because your vision and your options have expanded.

## The elements of trust

Strong, productive relationships can thrive only in an atmosphere of *trust*. Trust exists when each party can depend on the strength, honesty, integrity, and abilities of the other. Think of the people you know. Aren't there some people you are positive that you can count on for certain things? Aren't there others who you are just as positive that you can't count on?

)) Trusting relationships are built between people who have certain characteristics. For example, you trust people with *integrity*. In other words, you know that what they say is accurate and truthful. Integrity is usually established through experience with a person, but occasionally it is vouched for by a trusted authority or by reputation.

)) Another element of trust is *transparency*. Transparency is the complete absence of a hidden agenda, when all parties are aware of everything that needs to be known—the motives, opinions, and goals of everyone involved. Transparency precludes hiding behind jargon or legalese. Of course, legal language is sometimes necessary, but it should never be used to needlessly complicate or conceal information. Suspicion—the opposite of trust—can exist only when there is an absence of information. Complete and open communication creates transparency.

)) A third element of trust is *authenticity*, or the art of being yourself. Whatever you may think of yourself, you are absolutely great at being you—after all, you're the most qualified for the job. When you let your own personal light shine, others will be drawn to you. But when you cover that light by pretending to be something you're not, other people might wonder what you're up to. By being yourself, being authentic, you create the foundation upon which a trusting relationship can be built.

Whether in business or in your personal life, quality relationships depend on the level of trust that the participants have in each other. The higher the level of trust, the higher the quality of the relationship. Even with relationships in which interactions are on a superficial level, a minimal level of trust adds quality.

Participants in a trusting relationship derive more value from their dealings with each other. As I mentioned earlier, when a controversial topic is broached, neither person worries about sinister motives on the part of the other. The bedrock of trust ensures that they can have a discussion without worrying that the entire framework of the relationship will collapse.

For this reason, deep friendships usually take many years to mature and reach this level of trust. The patterns of trust have been built progressively, each person making small adjustments and compensations for the idiosyncrasies of the other. Lower levels of trust are built upon until the friendship stands firm. Time and effort provide strength and depth to a friendship.

The removal of doubt dramatically reduces the anxiety level of a relationship. When you can depend on the other person to show integrity and honesty, most potential worries are eliminated. Doubts are like acid in a relationship, eating away at both participants. With trust in place, doubts are kept to a minimum, so both parties are more relaxed and open.

How do you go about building trust? By being trustworthy—that is, being worthy of trust. You achieve this worthiness by adhering to traditional standards of honor. Be honest, keep your word, and show respect for the other person. These traits are under your complete control in a relationship. No one else has control over your honor.

The value you put on a relationship is shown by keeping your commitments to the other person. What you put before those commitments tells the other person where they stand with you. For example, let's say that you make a lunch date with a friend. A half hour before the appointed time, your boss asks you if you want to have lunch with him. No clients or business are involved—it's just the boss wanting to be sociable.

If you cancel the date with your friend, you are telling him that even an unimportant impromptu lunch with your boss takes precedence over your plans with him, If, on the other hand, you tell your boss that you have a prior appointment, your friend will know that you have placed your relationship with him above other options.

There is no chart or graph to determine when or under what circumstances you should keep or break a commitment to a friend. However, you have to realize that every broken commitment is a withdrawal from the emotional bank account, and too many withdrawals can destroy trust. Honoring commitments both large and small puts huge deposits in the account, and a relationship will flourish with that kind of investment.

The main thing to remember in any relationship is that trust cannot be assumed automatically. It must be earned. The only way to earn trust is to honor the relationship and to follow the fundamental principles of honor and integrity.

## Relationships

Obviously, the goal is to form *strong* relationships whenever possible. What is a strong relationship? It's one that acknowledges and survives the occasional failings of the human beings involved. As humans we are prone to vulnerability, weaknesses, and imperfections. Most of the disappointments we have in other people result when they fall short of our expectation that they will be perfect. Strong relationships survive the mistakes we make when people exhibit imperfect traits.

Vulnerabilities are the soft emotional spots in each of us. In a strong relationship, each partner is understanding and supports the other's vulnerability. For example, for those who have lost their parents, Mother's Day and Father's Day can be emotional times. They may express their emotions in bouts of anger, sadness, withdrawal, or a combination of these or other emotions. Understanding a person's vulnerability under these or similar circumstances reflects a strong relationship.

Emotions often express themselves indirectly. Through sincere interest in and caring about the other person, you can learn about and forgive these emotional expressions when they occur. A relationship is more than a single episode of less-than-perfect behavior. The best relationships survive these episodes.

Each of us also has both strengths and weaknesses. A strong relationship acknowledges each person's weaknesses and compensates for them. You don't expect your dog to be able to climb trees when you take him for a walk. He's not a cat. In the same way, if one person in a relationship lacks physical strength, the other neither expects nor asks that person to do something that would require great physical strength. You acknowledge that particular weakness.

Forgiveness of weaknesses does not mean that you put up with behavior that violates your beliefs or values. Remember, a strong relationship is based on having similar core values. If a friend engages in immoral behavior (based on the values that you believe you have in common), you should address the reason for that weakness. However, in a strong relationship, you care enough for the other person so that an unusual display of weakness does not threaten the relationship.

Likewise, when we have built a high level of trust, human imperfections don't threaten us. After all, life is full of unpredictable moments. A friend or acquaintance may break their word or fail to honor a commitment. With a high level of trust, our reaction is more likely to be "I wonder if they're okay" or "Something must have happened." We try to support the other person rather than cast blame.

We try to protect strong relationships that have a high level of trust. Although it's important to recognize the weaknesses, imperfections, and vulnerabilities of the other person, it's also important to be willing to accept his support when you show these same traits. You're human too, and although it's admirable to aim for perfection, it's not realistic. You will occasionally fall short yourself.

At such times, you need to be able to depend on the other person, not only in the sense that he is dependable, but also that you are honest enough with yourself to accept his help when offered. Pride is one of the worst killers of relationships—"pride goeth before a fall." When someone with whom you have a strong, quality relationship offers to help you, it's for the right motives.

## Sales relationships

I've hammered pretty hard on the essentials of strong, productive, quality relationships as they apply to everyone with whom we interact. For someone engaged in sales of any kind, those relationships are absolutely vital. Why are relationships the key to success in sales?

In his book *The SPEED of Trust: The One Thing That Changes Everything*, Stephen M. R. Covey (son of Stephen R. Covey) emphasizes that, in today's business world, rapidly building trust with clients, customers, and other stakeholders is a primary requisite for any business or organization aiming to perform at the highest levels.

On the most pragmatic level, customers prefer to do business with someone they like. If they derive pleasure from dealing with you, your sales are more likely to increase. If likeability were the only criteria, though, service, quality, and dependability wouldn't matter. Anyone who has been in business more than 10 minutes knows that's ridiculous. It takes much more than surface charm to obtain and keep a customer's business.

While building meaningful relationships takes time, it doesn't take much! The small, simple things make all the difference in your relationships with customers. Here are some quick tips about what you can do today to take your relationship and your business to the next level:

- Call a customer just to see what you can do for him.

- Send a handwritten congratulatory note to a customer who may have achieved something or been recognized.

- Have your staff call with a "Thanks for your business" message.

- Take a customer to lunch.

- Ask a customer for advice on a service or product issue.

- Send an unexpected bonus with a customer's order.

- Send a handwritten thank-you note for a customer's payment.

- Celebrate your customers' successes.

- Hold regular listening sessions with your customers.

This last point deserves special attention. In his book *In Search of Excellence*, business guru Tom Peters introduced the concept of MBWA—Managing by Wandering Around. It means that managers often benefit themselves and their companies more by speaking directly to customers and finding out their concerns, problems, gripes, and issues without the information filtered being through multiple layers of staff concerned with protecting their jobs.

When I led sales teams, I used a similar concept called *lobby management* (or what I preferred to call it, *lobby schmoozing*). I instructed my sales management staff to schedule times when they got out from behind their desks, left their offices, and spent time talking directly to customers. In this way they were able to get feedback about the customers' experiences, what we could do to better meet their needs, and what was on their minds.

Imagine if every management meeting started with a customer story— good or bad—about how the company had performed. Think of how the business culture would change if, from the top down, everyone in the organization was concerned with doing what's best for the customer.

You get the idea. Challenge yourself and your staff to discover new ways to deepen relationships with your customers or clients. As these relationships mature, so will your business. None of these gestures should cost you much in either money or time, but the message they send, and the relationships they help to forge, will be priceless.

Whatever the product or service that you choose to sell, the key to success is selling yourself. Your customers absolutely have to believe that you have their interests in mind when you approach them. If you follow the guidelines described earlier and show honesty, integrity, transparency, and dependability when dealing with them, they will be more receptive to the ideas you present.

Because those traits are so uncommon and even old-fashioned today, when you display such virtues, you will stand out from most of the people they know. *Quality* is the term that will come to mind, and quality people are always attractive. That is, other people will be attracted to you when you have shown your worth to them.

So although you always want to put your best foot forward when describing your product or service, never misrepresent or lie. Such actions poison a relationship, and when discovered, they destroy trust that can never be fully restored. When you place your customers' concerns at the same level as your own and commit to a win-win relationship, you set the bar high— and you should always strive to rise to that level.

Because of the part-business, part-personal relationship most salespeople have with their customers, it's even more important to have their concerns solidly in mind. How do you discover those concerns? You listen.

## )) Listening skills

Most people are extremely poor listeners. They are engaged in the most basic level of listening, what I call *internal listening* (Level 1). They may hear the words the other person says, but they don't listen for understanding. They are simply waiting for the chance to respond.

Have you ever caught your attention wandering when someone is speaking to you? This happens because, instead of paying attention to the other person, we pay attention to ourselves. We are so in love with the sound of our own voice and what we're going to say next that we often miss what the other person is trying to communicate.

In such cases we are primarily aware of our own:

- Thoughts

- Opinions

- Judgments

- Feelings

- Needs

- Itches

- Conclusions

Most of the time, if we give any indication that we're listening, we nod our heads and say "uh-huh" at what we consider the appropriate times. Inside, however, we are telling ourselves:

- I had an experience just like that.

- This is starting to bore me.

- I'm scared I will say the wrong thing and look stupid.

- I have my own opinion on this one.

When we listen at this level, we are unaware of the other person and unaware of our impact on that person.

Much more beneficial is *focused listening* (Level 2). At this level, you focus your attention sharply on the other person. You direct your listening to the person speaking. You listen closely to:

- Words

- Expressions

- Emotions

- Values

We listen as well for what people don't say and what energizes them. When you ask questions, do they come alive, or do they become withdrawn? At this level, we are listening holistically, regarding their words in the context of the situation, their experiences, and the purpose of the conversation. The message they are communicating takes place on many levels besides simply the words they use.

This leads to the concept of *global listening* (Level 3). At this level, you take in everything. You identify the energy between you and the speaker. Although you are aware of what is happening around you, you're not distracted from the other person's message. Your attention includes everything—what you see, what you hear, what you smell, what you feel.

At this level, you readily detect shifts in mood or attitude. You have greater access to your intuition, so the speaker can speak almost in shorthand. Single words or phrases describe entire situations and circumstances. Moreover, you become intensely aware of your impact on the speaker.

It almost goes without saying that the professional salesperson strives for global listening when talking to customers. If they express concerns, you should be capable of reading between the lines to detect whether there are really other, more serious matters behind their words. Addressing what's really on the customer's mind can often make the difference between making a sale or walking out the door empty-handed.

## Asking quality questions

The key to developing good listening skills is the ability to ask good questions. Questions should be used to clarify what the person has said. Quality questions lead to:

- Discovery
- Insight
- Deepening learning
- Action
- Commitment

The best way to obtain information is to ask open-ended questions—that is, questions that cannot be answered with a simple yes or no. The speaker is compelled to provide content and context when answering, giving you a better idea of what's behind the words and how he arrived at the conclusions he holds.

Quality questions can be asked only when you listen at Level 2 or Level 3. When you attend to the other person's agenda, you look to his needs. Remember the old axiom, "They don't care how much you know until they know how much you care." (See Chapter 7 for other powerful ways that you can use questions.)

Such questions are vital when you are engaged in *service recovery*. Service recovery occurs when something has gone wrong in the transaction between you and your customer. A shipment might have been late, the quality of your product or service may have fallen short, or any of a number of other problems. How you respond to such a situation is critical.

》You have to expect human lapses in business relationships from time to time. A business must have a Service Recovery Strategy—planned steps that correct errors and get service that has fallen short back on track, fast! With a strategy in place, when something does go off the rails, everyone knows who does what by when. Clear accountabilities are set, and specific people empowered to make right what went wrong. I cannot overemphasize the importance of people owning the responsibility to fix problem situations, whether they are the ones who created the problem or not.

Whoever first hears of a problem from a customer has to own the problem until it is fixed, or formally hand it off to another responsible colleague. Whoever hears of the problem from the customer must remember that they are the company in the eyes of the customer. The representation is critical in regaining the customer's confidence and loyalty.

Remember, your reaction makes all the difference in the relationship between you and the customer. If you try to hedge or avoid responsibility— especially if the fault was yours—your credibility immediately takes a nosedive. The first step is to take responsibility and to correct the situation as quickly as possible.

Your goal in such a situation (after resolving the issue) is to make sure that the relationship continues. If you have built a quality relationship with your customer, he will be more forgiving following a lapse on your or your company's part. He knows that he can count on you the rest of the time and that this occurrence was unusual. Respond professionally and maturely, and you can recover from the occasional problem.

It's vital that your organization or business respond immediately to situations in which the service or system has broken down. Correcting a situation before the customer even becomes aware of it is the best way to enhance your credibility with the customer. If the customer is already unhappy with you over an error, your immediate response is the only way to regain the credibility that you've lost, even if the loss was temporary.

A powerful and appropriate response can sometimes take the business relationship to new heights. The person or company responsible takes ownership of the error and fixes it so well that the customer is impressed to the point of being more committed to the relationship. They often will tell others about the problem they had and the prompt and professional way it was corrected.

When I was the Vice President of Sales and Service with Vancity Credit Union in Vancouver, BC, I empowered my staff to use their own judgment when resolving problems, regardless of the level at which it occurred. If the credit union erred, the staff member had automatic authorization to offer the customer something that would resolve the situation. The staff member might send flowers, movie passes, or—depending on how serious the error was—something more substantial, without having to wait on the chain of command.

I told my staff that we expected them to use their judgment as to the appropriate response to our error. For example, reimbursing an incorrect charge was automatic. At the same time, they knew not to send the customer on a two-week cruise simply because the credit union had made a mistake. They were expected to use their best judgment about what would resolve the issue and make sense to both parties. The response had to be good for the customer and also for the institution. I treated my staff as professionals and gave them my trust as to the appropriate response.

Many of these situations can be prevented if you manage the expectations of your customers. If you have any doubts, remember to always *underpromise and overdeliver*. There is a story of a flight that was on the runway, waiting to take off. The pilot announced that there would be a two-hour delay because of bad weather. The passengers groaned in anger and disappointment.

Fifteen minutes later, the pilot came back on and said that air traffic was moving faster than expected and that the delay was cut to only an hour. The passengers murmured approvingly—their wait had been cut in half. Fifteen minutes later, the pilot announced that, because of the quick adjustments, the flight would be leaving immediately. The passengers cheered as the plane readied for takeoff. They talked happily with one another as it took off. The pilot had underpromised and overdelivered.

Another great example of overdelivering is the Disney organization. I recently spent a summer vacation at Disneyland with my grandkids, and the lines—which I always dread at other places—were surprisingly pleasant. The waits were never as long as announced, and therefore guests were always happy and had a feeling of getting more than they had expected.

## Referrals

One of the hardest tasks of being a professional salesperson is *cold-calling*, or meeting potential clients with whom you have no relationship. You might think that top-level salespeople are experts at cold-calling, but the exact opposite is true. Experienced, successful salespeople almost never cold-call, because they have learned the power of *referrals*.

At its most basic, a referral is simply the name of a potential customer that you have received from a current customer. In the best cases, a current customer recommends or even introduces you to someone else who can benefit from your product or service. Your customer, who is familiar with what you sell and the quality of your service, has prequalified the referral, so you are engaged in the most effective activity possible for a salesperson—talking to someone who can use your product or service.

The single greatest compliment someone can pay a salesperson is sending them a personal referral. Lots of great companies never advertise—all of their business comes from referrals and word of mouth. The connection with their customers is stronger—and these firms are more profitable, because they don't have the expense of advertising. You can achieve this level only if your service fulfills the promise you make to the customer.

When I was a branch manager many years ago, I credited much of my business growth to the fact that my staff and I regularly gained new business by way of referrals from satisfied customers. These customers wanted to share their experiences with other people.

Very recently, I had yet another opportunity to make a business referral to help out a friend who is the CEO of a business. During a casual conversation, he mentioned some new directions that he had in mind for his company. I thought of acquaintances of mine who run a company called The Next Institute, a unique consulting firm that specializes in developing strong leaders and stimulating value creation. Their services would be ideal for my friend.

The Next Institute does no advertising, relying exclusively on referrals and word of mouth. I had heard some great things about them from executives at companies I respect with whom they had worked, so I had no qualms about connecting my friend with them. The partnership worked out wonderfully, and both parties were happy.

Because of their wonderful reputation and performance, I have since formed a great professional relationship with the folks at The Next Institute. I highly admire their attitude and their commitment to excellence.

This story is not unusual—it's exactly how referrals work. Information picked up in casual conversations leads to opportunity—but only if you work hard to deserve it.

As customers, we feel good when referring a great business or service to a friend, a family member, or a colleague. When that friend tells us how great his own experience was after following our referral, we feel good. Introducing our friends or family to someone we trust to serve them is risky unless there is a strong, trusting relationship. That's why, as a salesperson, you should treasure referrals and appreciate what your customer is entrusting you with. That only adds to the value of referrals to you.

## DECADES OF TRUST

Terry Jones, a branch manager with Envision Credit Union, knows something about referrals and customer loyalty through her own experience. She first met Barbara in 1988, while Terry was managing a branch of a local credit union. Barbara was a single woman who wanted to obtain a loan to purchase a business. As Terry worked with her, she realized that Barbara represented many female customers she had had over the years.

Women often find themselves suddenly single—widowed or divorced—and at a loss as to how to handle their finances, having often left that responsibility to someone else. Terry worked with many such women, coaching them on how to increase and manage wealth, and otherwise providing guidance on how to get out of financial hardship (which many of the women, suddenly on their own, found themselves suffering). Terry provided not only financial advice but also encouragement and education.

Barbara had not been able to get a loan at other banks, so because Terry had helped her, she kept Terry as her banker when she moved to other branches, even when Terry switched institutions, moving to what eventually became Envision Credit Union.

Terry has since helped Barbara's children, and even her grandchildren, with their financial needs. Not only that, but Barbara has referred countless numbers of people to Terry because of the trust she has in Terry's guidance and commitment to customer service. Terry Jones knows firsthand how much a strong relationship can help everyone involved.

Think about it. Not only are you spending your valuable time in the best way, but you are also getting a solid recommendation from someone who already has credibility with your potential client. Can you see why top sales professionals do everything they can to maximize their referrals?

When you have gone to lengths to develop quality relationships with your customers, asking them for referrals is simple. You have established yourself as a key service source, and in such cases, they are keen to give you names of people who might use your product or service, and to recommend you to those people.

The key to getting referrals? Asking. You have established yourself in the relationship as someone having the virtues that mark you as a quality person and a quality service provider. You have listened to your customers at the deepest level. When you serve your customers well, they will brag to others about you. Referrals are the lifeblood of any professional salesperson. Strong relationships form the bond that will make your customers happy to help you.

# CHAPTER 4
## The Super Power You Already Have

THERE ARE SOME PEOPLE WHO LIVE
IN A DREAM WORLD, AND THERE ARE
SOME WHO FACE REALITY; AND THEN
THERE ARE THOSE WHO TURN ONE
INTO THE OTHER.

–Douglas Everett

# CHAPTER 4
## The Super Power You Already Have

Do you have any idea how truly amazing you are? You are blessed with the most powerful calculating machine ever created—the human brain. It's been estimated that the human brain contains as many as 100 billion cells, called neurons, each of which is connected to other neurons via electrical charges called synapses. The brain has as many as 500 trillion synapses, enabling the brain to process millions of bits of data.

With such an instrument available to each of us, it's no wonder that experts have worked for hundreds of years to figure out exactly how the brain works. Although they have been able to map out the physical structure of the brain, scientists still have not been able to uncover all the workings of the human mind. It is still the most complex and mysterious aspect of how and why human beings do what they do.

They have been able to determine that anything we do, anything we create, is created in the mind first. You think about cooking dinner, and then you do it. You think about drawing a picture, and then you do it. For everything humanity has ever created, there were actually two creations—one in the mind and then one in the physical world.

Following that concept, if you want to create a successful life for yourself, you first have to create it in your mind. Harnessing the power of your mind is one of the most important skills you can learn, fundamental to everything else you want to accomplish. How do you go about doing so?

## The conscious and the subconscious minds

Although the brain—the physical organ housed inside your skull—has been mapped out, scientists have not been able to pinpoint that part that constitutes your mind. Fortunately, we don't have to wait for a map in order to be able to use our minds. Practical experience has taught experts in human motivation that we have to gain control over only two things—our conscious mind and our subconscious mind.

)) The *conscious mind* is the thinking mind, the part where we go to access information. The information we get there influences our thoughts, and our thoughts determine our feelings and therefore our actions. If you want to go on vacation, you decide where you want to go based on information you've gathered from such sources as friends, television, movies, and the Internet. You then figure out how to get there. Based on that information, you decide to fly, to drive, or to find some other form of transportation to take you to that spot.

How does the conscious mind work? It deals with ideas. When presented with an idea, the conscious mind either accepts, rejects, or neglects the idea. The decision we make about which of those courses to take depends on our viewpoint, established by the programming we have received (whether faulty or not) and our life experiences. Our judgments are affected by those factors.

To render a decision, the conscious mind compares the idea to previous circumstances, so it has some sort of context, acting as a filter in a way. If the idea is similar to something that has occurred before, we are likely to judge the current idea based on the previous one. If the previous experience was pleasurable, we accept the idea. If it was painful, we reject the idea.

If the idea is unique, or brand new, the conscious mind will often completely reject the idea, refusing to accept it. This is often the reason for confusion when we don't understand something. Without a reference point to anchor the new idea to, the mind struggles at putting the idea into some sort of context.

Those people we consider geniuses are those who are able to make connections between new ideas and previous ones. Often the connection is not apparent to other people. Finding a particular, often subtle similarity between two otherwise disparate ideas is what we call "inspiration" or "a flash of genius." It is the conscious mind working at a higher level.

The conscious mind communicates and receives information from the world through the senses. If we want to communicate with the world, we use methods that stimulate the senses of another person. We speak so that someone else can hear our thoughts. We write, so someone else can read (see) our thoughts.

Much of the information available to the conscious mind is ignored; otherwise, we wouldn't be able to process all of it. Hundreds, if not thousands, of pieces of information come to us through our senses. Paying attention to more than a few of these details would be so distracting that we wouldn't be able to function.

The conscious mind develops from the time we are small children. At first we are essentially blank slates, unable to form judgments. Everything we perceive through our senses is new, so we have no context with which to judge anything. As we grow older, however, we begin to make judgments based on our limited experiences. Because of the small number of experiences, many of our judgments are in error. For example, a child may see something that appears to have many legs and assume it's a spider. It may be a shadow or a wad of thread or something else. However, the child has made her judgments based on what she's seen before.

At this time, we begin forming the belief systems we carry with us the rest of our lives. Because our judgment is fallible, especially as children, many of our belief systems are built on erroneous judgments. Our conscious mind has developed but with mistakes. However, with effort we can change our conscious mind and eliminate those misconceptions.

Because most of us live in a reasonably safe environment, our conscious mind does not have to work at 100 percent capacity for us to function throughout the day. Depending on the circumstances, various situations require us to use a bit more or a bit less at any given time. Experts agree that human beings use only about 10 percent of their potential brainpower.

Some people train themselves to use more of their minds. For example, botanists walk through a forest and notice various plants that non-botanists miss. Wildlife experts see tracks and other signs of the passage of animals that non-experts miss. They have trained themselves to use more of their conscious minds to achieve certain goals.

Experienced salespeople do something similar. They may overhear a conversation about a customer's event and immediately connect products and services that could benefit the customer's experience. Good salespeople look for "tracks" and other signs that indicate an opportunity for their company to add value to another person's life.

In contrast to the conscious mind, which exerts judgment on ideas, the *subconscious mind* works on a more universal, emotional level. The conscious mind expresses itself via the senses, whereas the subconscious uses feelings and emotions to communicate.

))) Unlike the conscious mind, the subconscious mind cannot judge the information it is presented with. Everything, whether real or imagined, is believed. It can't differentiate between the two. For example, we understand that movies are invented stories about invented characters. The people we see on the screen are actors. Yet moviemakers are masters at creating various emotions in the audience, from fear to anger to sadness. Have you ever watched a movie that made you cry? Your subconscious, your emotional mind, believed what it saw on the screen, even though your conscious mind knew that it was all fiction.

The subconscious mind is also attuned to *vibrations*. Vibrations are impressions of our experiences that cannot be discerned through the senses. We use particular language to describe those impressions. Most of us have had experiences that we could only describe as having a "good vibe" or a "bad vibe." When things go well and everything seems to fall in place, we speak of there being "harmony." Something familiar "strikes a chord."

Every situation has vibrations, and when your personal vibration matches the situation, things go well. You meet another person and hit it off right away—your vibrations are aligned. The problem is that the rest of the world also has vibrations, and they don't always match yours. When the world's vibrations influence your situation, nothing seems to go right.

It's important to understand that your subconscious mind understands vibrations, even if your conscious mind can't articulate what's happening. Perhaps you're dealing with a customer, and suddenly you simply get the feeling that something has changed during the conversation. You can't quite put your finger on it, but the vibration has changed, and your subconscious mind communicates with you to let you know. Perhaps you touched on a subject that was sensitive, or the customer's mood was affected by an outside source. The subconscious is hard at work.

Remember, the subconscious mind accepts whatever idea it is given. True or not, an idea will plant itself in the subconscious and continue to exert its influence for as long as it can. When we are young, these ideas are implanted and become our belief systems, which in turn cause us to make certain decisions under certain circumstances for the rest of our lives.

As you can imagine, your belief systems exert tremendous power over the quality of your life. As children we didn't have the power or the resources to control the images that our subconscious mind took in. Every impression, every emotion, every trauma resulted in our forming a particular image and belief that we simply accepted as true.

Even when the facts have changed, rendering the belief inaccurate, our subconscious still regards it as true. For example, a person might have been overweight as a child, resulting in taunts from schoolmates. Children can be mercilessly cruel, and such taunts often have a huge impact on the person's self-esteem. Parents, wishing to be helpful, may have tried to coerce the child into activities to help him lose weight, thus reinforcing the message. The child formed the mental belief that he was "fat."

Now the child has grown into an adult. Through lifestyle changes or simply by maturing, the adult is now slender. However, he may still carry the self-image of being fat. Despite the changed facts, the adult may still worry about how he looks, be self-conscious about his eating habits, and even become socially awkward because of the fear of being taunted. The subconscious mind has determined the direction of his entire life. The self-image is still that of the fat child.

Another factor that gives the subconscious mind such power is that it is always working. On one hand, it regulates the body's response to sensations. A particular image may make us happy. The feel of a scratchy sweater irritates us. A smell may remind us of another situation. The sensations that come to us via our senses are filtered through emotional experience.

Besides the connection to the physical world, the subconscious mind also works at reinforcing the beliefs it already holds. We may read a headline and automatically agree or disagree with it, based on what we already believe. The human inclination is to seek out points of view that agree with our personal beliefs. The subconscious mind continually compares our experiences in the world with those beliefs and evaluates them accordingly.

## Harnessing the mind's power

With the tremendous influence our mind has on us, how do we go about making it work for us rather than against us? The first step is to understand the process by which we achieve results in our lives. Our goals are to produce more of the results we want and fewer of the results we don't want.

Achieving our goals starts with the powerful subconscious mind. A thought or a situation stimulates a feeling, an emotion. Based on those feelings, we take particular actions. Those actions, in turn, produce results, both good and bad, intended and unintended. The actions may even be contrary to what our conscious mind knows we ought to do. The subconscious is simply too strong.

When the results are not what we want, we wind up asking ourselves that age-old question, *Why do I do things that I know I shouldn't do?* or its fraternal twin, *Why don't I do the things I know I should do?* Now you know the answer. You made the decision to take particular actions based on what your often undependable subconscious mind told you.

To harness the power of your subconscious mind, think of it as a garden. For most people, that garden is full of weeds—the weeds of mistaken beliefs: *I'm too fat, I'm too thin, I'm too old, I'm too young.* The weeds are plentiful. You have to begin by weeding your garden.

Unlike physical weeds, you can't simply pull the weeds out of your subconscious mind. The mind abhors a vacuum, and if there is nothing to replace the beliefs you remove, they will simply grow back. To bring your subconscious mind back to a useful state—our metaphorical "clean garden"—you have to replace those beliefs with new, more productive ones.

Remember that the subconscious believes everything it's told. The process is simple—you simply give your subconscious mind the images you want to believe. The more often you repeat the image, the greater hold it will take. For example, if you want to achieve success, you have to saturate your mind with images of success. Read inspiring books, find stories of people who have achieved success—anything that equates to success, to you.

This step is simple to describe but sometimes difficult to put into practice consistently. Our old belief systems always want to exert their influence on us. It takes conscious effort—using the conscious mind—to realize that we are falling back into old patterns and to change our actions when that happens. Remember, if you want to change the results you're getting, you have to change your actions, and that can only happen after you change your thoughts.

Think of your negative patterns of belief and behavior as old friends that you've outgrown. They show up sometimes unexpectedly, and they're always unwelcome. Simply acknowledge them and insert your new positive images in their place. Eventually the old patterns will get the message and quit coming around. To change your results, change what you think about.

## The body/mind connection

If you ever have any doubt about the mind's effects on the body, try speaking in front of a group. Public speaking consistently ranks at or near the top in surveys of our greatest fears. Most people, when asked to speak before a group, feel their heart race, their mouth grow dry, their stomach churn unpleasantly, and their breathing become shallow and fast. They are in no physical danger, yet the body reacts the same way as our ancestors' did when face to face with a predator.

As I mentioned earlier, the emotions we experience are caused by associations created from the programming we learn from childhood. These emotions may or may not gel into complete thoughts, but at some point the emotion will manifest itself into a physical sensation. As with public speaking, sometimes the sensations are unpleasant. At other times, they may be more pleasant. For example, perhaps childhood memories of the aroma of food cooking in your mother's kitchen trigger a warm feeling in the stomach.

Memories then can clearly cause emotions and physical reactions. What about non-existent situations? People who have phobias, such as the fear of heights, may experience all the sensations of being in a fearful situation simply by imagining it. They may even get dizzy and have to sit down to recover. When the mind chooses, it can exert tremendous pressure on the body.

What does this have to do with success? It applies for a couple of reasons. First, if some thoughts provoke pleasure while others cause pain, we will naturally try to have more of those thoughts that bring us pleasure and fewer of those that cause pain. We move away from pain toward pleasure.

The mind can be very shortsighted, however. It may be necessary to go through temporary discomfort to achieve a higher level of pleasure. For example, exercise can be physically uncomfortable, even painful, at times. Left on its own, the mind would try to move you away from this pain.

The conscious mind, however, understands that physical exercise can improve your quality of life and help you live longer. Going through temporary pain, then, leads to a greater pleasure. You override the mind's first impulse to achieve the goal you desired. Most people who exercise regularly eventually come to enjoy it, and the mind's painful associations are eliminated.

One thing we know for sure is that successful people are usually willing to do things that less successful people won't do. They may work extra hours, cold-call on a new prospect, or forego leisure time to attend school or workshops. There is temporary pain associated with these activities, but high achievers understand that a greater pleasure awaits them.

It's much easier and more pleasant (at least for some people) to clock out at five o'clock, go home, eat dinner, and sit in front of the television the rest of the night than to make a few more calls on clients after everyone else has gone home for the day. Choosing a temporary pain that leads to a long-term pleasure is a sign of maturity and the way to achieve more success.

Second, the mind's ability to create pleasurable sensations can be a motivator only if it's done properly. In Chapter 2, I presented this advice: aim for a goal that excites you a lot and scares you only a little. Very often, goals are imposed on us by other people, either directly or by peer pressure. All members of a sales team may shoot for $100,000 a year in commissions. This goal may be fine, but it may also hurt one or more members.

Think about it—the goal represents both pleasure (excites you) and pain (scares you). The particular dollar amount that excites you a lot and scares you only a little is unique to you. Your childhood, your current circumstances, or any number of other factors determine how the amount affects you.

In the same way, any ambitious goal can affect you emotionally, actually hurting performance, because the excitement is outweighed by the fear. Your mind finds a way to work against the very thing you want to achieve. Choose your goals carefully and pay attention to the emotions and physical sensations they evoke.

Within the closed system of the mind and body, the mind rules. What the mind decides, the body must carry out. However, remember that the instrument that houses the mind—the brain—is a physical part of the body, and therefore obeys natural laws regarding the body. For example, if you don't get enough quality sleep, your mind may be sluggish. Decisions will be hard to make, and you'll get confused about facts.

Similarly, diet and exercise are both just as important to the mind as to the body. Poor nutrition or a deteriorating body can disrupt good thinking. The mind depends on the body for nourishment, and you can literally starve your mind. Although the mind is the ruler of the body, the mind also depends on the body to sustain it.

In the same way, the mind can affect the body's ability to fight disease, infection, and pain. Study after study has shown how negative thoughts undermine the body's ability to protect itself. Conversely, positive thinking can actually boost your immune system and help you ward off disease and infection.

The medical community has focused massive amounts of attention on the *placebo effect.* The placebo effect occurs when a patient believes that he is receiving treatment and starts responding favorably—whether he actually has received the treatment or not. Most common is when a patient is given sugar pills for a particular medical condition, and the condition improves. Medical researchers have even discovered that a particular color of placebo pills works on one condition, whereas another color is better for another.

Additionally, we've all known people who seemed to have a higher-than-usual tolerance for physical pain. They have conditioned their minds to disregard the pain—for whatever reason—so lower levels of pain no longer affect them. You might see this effect in a kitchen where the cooks barely notice the minor burns that come with dealing with hot foods, or on a construction site where workers use large tools, sometimes accidentally banging them against their arms or legs. They have learned to ignore minor pains in their "culture."

My daughter Tracey recently ran her first marathon, in Vancouver. Prior to the race, she trained for months, waking early in the morning when it was still dark, often running in the snow. Getting into marathon-level condition was painful, but she pushed back the pain because she was so focused on her goal.

During the race, her feet became sore, which she had expected. But she also knew that her toes were bleeding, because the blood was leaking through her runners. The months of conditioning her mind to ignore physical discomfort enabled her to put the pain out of her mind and focus on finishing the marathon.

In another case, I made the personal commitment to complete the Grouse Grind (a popular hike up the 2,800-foot vertical side of Grouse Mountain in Vancouver) five times in one day. I generally do the challenging climb once a day as a form of exercise.

I knew it would be a very difficult day of climbing, so I forced myself to stay focused on completing my goal. I ignored the discomfort of the heat, tiredness, leg cramps, and nausea. It was truly mind over matter—my mind was in control, not my body.

This mentality is analogous to that of the high achievers mentioned earlier. What other people might consider pain or discomfort, the achievers don't even register. They have trained their minds to accept the sensations and pursue their goals regardless. How we experience the challenge is all in our perception.

The goal, of course, is to house a healthy mind inside a healthy body. For those who aspire to the highest levels of achievement, taking care of the two primary tools is the key to success. The mind-body connection is a deep subject, but discussing it in depth would take up the entire book. There are many other wonderful books that address this topic, and I encourage you to pursue the matter further.

# CHAPTER 5
## FLEXING YOUR MUSCLE

YOUR IMAGINATION IS THE PREVIEW
TO LIFE'S COMING ATTRACTIONS.

–Albert Einstein

# CHAPTER 5
## FLEXING YOUR MUSCLE

In the previous chapter, you learned that you, as a human being and as a salesperson, have immense power already at your disposal. As any reader of comic books can tell you, putting your super powers to good use takes training. Before we start with this training, understand this: you have the ability to change your reality. Whatever may have happened to you up to now, you alone can decide that you have the choice of how your life, in many areas, will develop from now on.

In one of my favorite books, *The 7 Habits of Highly Effective People*, Stephen R. Covey discusses the option that every person has: the ability to choose how to respond to outside stimuli. Most people go through life simply reacting to whatever hits them at any given time. Another driver cuts you off in traffic, and you get angry. A customer says no to your sales presentation, and you treat it as a defeat. Your significant other gives you a disapproving look, and you become sad. All of these are simple stimulus-reaction transactions.

What separates the enlightened person, says Covey, is that he *chooses* how he will respond to the outside world. The random actions of the world and of other people don't affect how he feels or how he will respond. If a customer says no to an offer, the enlightened salesperson *chooses* to take the refusal as part of the standard sales process and moves to the next customer with full confidence and energy. The driver who is cut off in traffic reacts safely and continues to hum the song he was singing in the shower.

Consciously making such choices, rather than letting random events dictate your mood, gives back control over your own life. The worst feeling in the world is that of powerlessness, of lacking control over your own life. Unfortunately, as Henry David Thoreau wrote, "The mass of men lead lives of quiet desperation." They neglect the choice that they are given, the choice to change their own lives.

Once you have made the decision to take back control of your life, you are ready to begin using your six intellectual faculties.

## )) The six intellectual faculties

Your intellectual faculties are the powers of your mind that you already have available. They are:

- Perception

- Will

- Memory

- Intuition

- Reason

- Imagination

You'll likely recognize these terms, but perhaps not in a way that you have put to use up to now. You will be stronger in some of these faculties, whereas others may need development. Everyone has all of them to one degree or another, but few people understand how they can help you improve your life.

))) *Perception* is the ability to understand something—not only in the school sense but in a way that may be contrary to what your senses are telling you. For example, your senses tell you that a young girl was carried away by a tornado to a land called Oz. Your perception lets you understand that you are watching a movie, and that it's not happening in real life. (Even when movies are based on actual events, your mind perceives that what you are seeing is not the event itself.)

Perception also reflects your point of view. If you look at any occurrence objectively, you find that it has many facets, and each person's knowledge of the event is based on their unique experience, programming, and beliefs. The Indian fable of the blind men and the elephant, best known in the West from a nineteenth-century poem, is based on the principle of perception:

## THE BLIND MEN AND THE ELEPHANT

By John Godfrey Saxe
It was six men of Indostan
To learning much inclined,
Who went to see the Elephant
(Though all of them were blind),
That each by observation
Might satisfy his mind

The First approached the Elephant,
And happening to fall
Against his broad and sturdy side,
At once began to bawl:
"God bless me! but the Elephant
Is very like a wall!"

The Second, feeling of the tusk,
Cried, "Ho! what have we here
So very round and smooth and sharp?
To me 'tis mighty clear
This wonder of an Elephant
Is very like a spear!"

The Third approached the animal,
And happening to take

The squirming trunk within his hands,
Thus boldly up and spake:
"I see," quoth he, "the Elephant
Is very like a snake!"

The Fourth reached out his eager hand,
And felt about the knee.
"What most this wondrous beast is like
Is mighty plain," quoth he;
"'Tis clear enough the Elephant
Is very like a tree!"

The Fifth, who chanced to touch the ear,
Said: "E'en the blindest man
Can tell what this resembles most;
Deny the fact who can,
This marvel of an Elephant
Is very like a fan!"

The Sixth no sooner had begun
About the beast to grope,
Then, seizing on the swinging tail
That fell within his scope,
"I see," quoth he, "the Elephant
Is very like a rope!"

And so these men of Indostan
Disputed loud and long,
Each in his own opinion
Exceeding stiff and strong,
Though each was partly in the right,
And all were in the wrong!

It is impossible to experience life completely objectively. We each have our own particular likes and dislikes. However, considering issues and situations from another point of view is sometimes helpful, opening up possibilities or alternatives that you may not have considered previously. Like the blind men of the fable, having a different perspective may help you more accurately assess the situation.

From this point, it's a small step to realize that the events in our world are neither good nor bad, right nor wrong, but are colored only by our own perception. The events themselves are neutral. However, they can provide useful information so that we can proceed more effectively in the future.

Rather than taking a situation as a success or failure, use what happens as feedback for your next step. Did what happened move you closer to your goals? If not, change what you did and try something different. Does it work now? No? Then try something different. The ability to use feedback from a situation to change your strategy is a sign of a top performer in any field.

For example, if you make a sales presentation to a potential customer who then says no, your perception may be negative—*he hates me, I'm worthless, I'm no good at sales, I'll never sell anything*—based on how your programming has affected you in the past. But if you change your perspective, you can listen to clues the customer gives you rather than to the negative voice in your head.

For example, the customer may have an issue with price. Instead of taking the rejection personally, you consider what the customer has said—change your perspective—and determine 1) whether the price is the real objection, and 2) whether there is a way you can overcome this objection. You take control of your situation by changing your perception, converting the information the customer has given you from a personal rejection to a normal part of the sales process.

If a situation has great emotional significance for you, you may become entrenched in your own perception and viewpoint, even though retaining your objectivity would be more effective. Experienced salespeople know that a big sale carrying a big commission is often the hardest presentation to give, simply because so much rides on it.

Consider this—if you put a four-inch-wide board on the ground, you would have no problem walking on it comfortably. Move it off the ground a foot, and you probably could still easily walk any distance on it. You're relaxed, and you know that stepping off would be no problem. Put the same board 60 feet in the air, and suddenly the consequences of failing become much more severe. Your fear makes it more difficult to walk any distance on the board.

The board hasn't changed. The only thing that has changed is your perception of the situation. If you can put aside your fears and concentrate on the matter at hand—something that you've done successfully before—then the task itself becomes easier, and you increase your chances for success.

))) *Will* is the ability to focus on the task at hand and on your overall plan. Will is the only force that can put into action all your other attributes. It's the intellectual faculty that allows you to stay firm in the face of all the obstacles and distractions that assault you daily. Without will, your life would be like a race car stuck at the starting line, revving its engine but never going anywhere.

Although you can make a habit of exhibiting will (or "willpower," as it is often called), ultimately, every moment belongs to you. You have the choice of whether to continue with your plan or to address another issue. This choice is called free will—a concept introduced to many of us early in life in the form of religious or spiritual training. As a human being, you are not locked in to any course of action. You can adapt as you choose.

Although we understand that staying focused on a task is the path to success, sometimes complete focus is undesirable. For example, if you are working at home, and one of your children runs into your office crying and bleeding, you would be cold-hearted indeed not to stop what you're doing and attend to the child's injury. The ability to refocus for a moment to address a higher priority is what makes us human.

For most of us, however, the problem is not *too much* focus. In today's electronic culture of 24-hour news, social networking websites such as Facebook and MySpace, Twitter, cell phones that constantly update us with what's happening in our world, and the Internet itself, it's the rare person who is not occasionally distracted. We struggle to keep these tools from squandering our time and drawing us away from our goals.

*Focus* is concentrating our energies in a way that moves us forward, toward our goals. Bob Proctor, a world-renowned personal development coach, says, "The will is to the mind as a magnifying glass is to the sun." The immense power of our conscious and subconscious minds must be directed toward a particular goal in order for that power to be effective. Just as a magnifying glass can burn a hole in a piece of paper with its intense light, your will is the light that guides you toward your dreams.

Using your will allows you to advance your perceptions and your self-image. The powers you have allow you to perceive more than your senses tell you, but only if you use those powers. You may have lived a good part of your life up to now allowing your intellectual faculties to remain dormant, closing your mind to opportunities that surround you.

Imagine how your self-image will change when you start using all your energies to accomplish your goals. Whereas before you might have berated yourself for a lackadaisical outlook, now you are "being all you can be." Fulfilling your potential is one of the greatest enhancers of self-image.

Another way that we lose focus or will is by looking ahead too much. There are times to plan, to brainstorm, or to strategize, and there are times simply *to do*. By being in the now, you ensure that you are giving your full efforts to accomplishing what you want to accomplish. If you have planned properly beforehand, you should not be distracted by worrying about the results or consequences of what you do.

Basketball great Michael Jordan was asked once about handling the pressure of taking a last-second shot during a big game. He shrugged the question off. There was no pressure, he said. But aren't you worried that you might miss? Jordan was puzzled. "Why would I worry about missing a shot that I haven't taken yet?"

Jordan, considered by many to be the greatest basketball player ever, was also known for his tremendous work ethic. He had taken thousands, if not hundreds of thousands, of practice shots, preparing him for that moment in a big game when he had the chance to score a basket and win the game. His will was tempered by all those hours of practice, so he didn't allow himself to be distracted by the pressure or by worrying.

You can follow his example and focus on the present moment, confident that the preparation you have done is sufficient to see you through the current task. Approach each day and each moment as full of opportunity. Exhibit the will that brings all your powers to bear on what is in front of you.

For many people, *memory* is simply the retention of information. Your ability to store and recall facts or situations that you have been exposed to in the past is a fundamental part of your human experience. From childhood experiences to what you had for breakfast, memory makes up a large part of what you rely upon to simply get through the day.

To a high achiever, though, the intellectual faculty of memory is much more than a simple recall of events. Memory is used to evaluate situations on several levels. It's the difference between seeing a great work of art as simply another picture and having the insight to appreciate the workmanship, themes, and beauty of the art itself. Memory gives context to our lives.

The philosopher George Santayana once wrote, "Those who cannot remember the past are condemned to repeat it." A simple recall of the past without learning from it—the level of memory that most people use—explains why we often make mistakes we shouldn't make.

We receive programming from many sources throughout our lives, much of it destructive. If you are in a situation in which you've previously had little or no success, plain memory will force you into the same course of action you took then. Using memory as an intellectual faculty, however, allows you to evaluate earlier results and adapt your actions as necessary to be successful.

If you spend your time dwelling on less favorable situations, you will become paralyzed. You will constantly remind yourself of how you failed. Dwelling on such memories ignores your ability to change and adapt. At these times, your memory plays false with you, defeating you before you even start.

It's much more effective to focus on positive memories, on times you achieved success, to counteract the negative programming you have received. Memories of times you accomplished something are more "true" than negative memories, because they reflect the resources you have at your disposal. You have the capacity to succeed in your life because you learned from previous experiences.

Thinking of your memory as a sort of mental muscle helps you develop the ability to control it. We see this analogy in practice all the time. Actors learn page after page of lines from a script. Musicians know dozens, sometimes hundreds, of pieces of music. Chess masters are able to play entire games without seeing the board or pieces. They have developed their memories to the extent that they are able to perform near-miraculous feats of memory.

Train yourself to use your memory productively. If you realize that you're dwelling on a negative memory, use your conscious mind to immediately stop. (Some people go so far as to literally shout "Stop!" when they find themselves stewing. I say "CANCEL!" out loud. It works for me. Do whatever works.) Find positive memories to replace the negative ones. The mindset to achieve success in one area can transfer to another area. Note that I'm not talking about specific skills, but the winning attitude you accessed on one occasion is available to you now.

Your memory is perfect. Most people have a negative idea of their own memory skills, but that's simply because they haven't developed their abilities. Everything is imprinted on the memory, and you choose which memories to access. Make memory work for you rather than against you.

*Intuition* is the intellectual faculty that keeps you from being ruled strictly by your five senses. It's going with your gut at those times that your rational, conscious mind argues against your decision. Because our rational mind usually overrules our intuition, the ability to respond to intuition has attained something of a mystical quality, yet it's anything but.

)))Intuition is the connection between your conscious and subconscious minds. Often, when we are attuned to the vibrations of a situation, the subconscious mind picks up on clues that the senses miss. The conscious mind is unable to articulate what's happening, but the subconscious mind knows, and it communicates in the only way it can—feelings.

Haven't you ever talked with someone and immediately gotten an impression of that person? You may call it chemistry or some other word, but your subconscious is telling you something. The heroes of the *Star Wars* movies repeated the line "I have a bad feeling about this" when they were about to go into a dangerous situation. As a society, we have become used to talking about using intuition in our lives.

## A STORY ABOUT TRUST AND INTUITION

I do a lot of work with Envision Credit Union. I enjoy working with them because, despite having thousands of member/customers and billions of dollars in assets, they still "get it" when it comes to values, integrity, sales, and building strong trusting relationships with their members. Let me share a story about how they placed their banking smarts aside to allow their heart smarts to do some of their decision making.

Natasha and Vladimir Bolshakov, a couple from the Ukraine, immigrated to the Vancouver area a few years ago. The Bolshakovs had a dream, a vision of how to use the master's degrees in engineering they had earned in their homeland and transform their knowledge into something new in North America. They wanted to manufacture acoustical panels, large screen-like panels as might be used in a library or a concert hall to improve overall sound quality.

The Bolshakovs' dream was one like most, creating something for the future and knowing they wouldn't be able to do it on their own. They needed financial support. Getting that support while new in the country, with minimal assets to show in a bank account, was their first challenge. Their assets—their engineering backgrounds and their vivid picture of what could be—were all in their heads.

The Bolshakovs knocked on Envision's door. They had a hunch that a credit union might be a good partner in helping them realize their dream. They met with Dwight Folk, a business account manager who knew they needed small-business expertise. The Bolshakovs introduced Dwight to their vision, Geometrik Manufacturing Inc. He listened well, and before long saw the same vision as Natasha and Vladimir. Natasha said this was their greatest gift in the whole process—meeting someone who could see what they saw.

Dwight was able to set aside all the normal criteria to see their vision and make his decision on what could be, instead of simply what was in front of him on paper. Most bankers would look for a borrowing track record, security, business earnings and equity, net worth, and more. The Bolshakovs had none of those. Dwight's intuition told him to take the chance and defy the lending criteria. He went with his gut and gave them a small line of credit, enough to launch their project. Natasha told me later that it was Dwight's *trust* that inspired them. He looked first at their trustworthiness, then at their business plan and projections. Dwight was able to see beyond the numbers to create a two-way, trusting relationship, one that Natasha says is their most important business relationship to this day.

Years later, that line of credit has grown and multiplied many times over. Geometrik Manufacturing is sought after for magazines, TV spots, and leading technology news articles. Natasha and Vladimir Bolshakov have created many specialized sound systems and have become the North American experts in this field. Thanks in part to Dwight Folk's intuition, they are living their dream.

When your conscious, rational mind is telling you to take a particular course of action, but your intuition indicates another, stop for a moment and contemplate what's happening. Ask yourself, *Why do I feel this way? Why is my subconscious trying to get my attention?* Often, you will discover that one of your fundamental values is being violated in subtle ways that are not readily apparent. Be alert for those occasions and be aware of what your intuition is telling you.

There are dangers in relying on your intuition, however. Intuition can sometimes send you in the wrong direction because of bad programming. For example, an opportunity arises that can move you closer to success, but your gut tells you to run away. This reaction can be simple fear or a lack of confidence, inserted into your life by programming you should have discarded long ago.

When you feel yourself at the point of running away from success, stop and consider the situation. Does the opportunity align with your values? Does it move you closer to success in an ethical way? Closing yourself off from avenues to succeed is a sign that bad programming is trying to assert itself via your subconscious. At such times, your intuition is not to be trusted.

On the other hand, on those occasions when you have looked at a situation, and your rational mind tries to control you, use your intuition to see if another course of action *feels* right. When it does, take the leap of faith and follow the path that your conscious mind has not thoroughly mapped.

))) After reading the previous section, you might have a negative view of your ability to reason. Don't. Most people spend the majority of their time using the reasoning part of the mind, and that's natural—it's what separates human beings from animals. Other creatures on the planet respond only to the information provided to them by their senses. Mankind has developed the ability to override merely sensual information to use logic.

For example, if a dog is hungry and food is present, he will eat it regardless of what it is. A human might be hungry but realizes that what's immediately available—chips, fried foods, candy—is bad for him nutritionally. He will delay eating until a more appropriate meal is available. The human can delay gratification in order to meet a larger goal.

The ability to reason depends on knowledge and education—not necessarily from a school but from some source. The application of knowledge gained in the past guides our decision making today. Formal education is fine for many areas of decision making, as long as the person was truly educated and didn't simply mark time until graduation. The accumulation of knowledge is never a bad thing.

Mere accumulation of knowledge for its own sake, however, is wasteful. Knowledge must be accessible and applied to appropriate situations. Creative reasoning is the ability to access information in unique ways that can be applied to a variety of situations. Analysis of situations or problems so that appropriate actions can be taken is the essence of reasoning and logic.

A character from the old television show *Cheers* was notable for his ability to recall useless bits of trivia. While it's admirable to have access to that much information, the character was unable to put any of it to good use. (After all, he spent a large amount of his time in a bar!) We all know someone who could be described as clever but who has not found a way to apply that intelligence to the real world. While sometimes entertaining—and often irritating—such individuals would be well advised to find a way to apply knowledge in a more useful way.

Reason, then, is a remarkable intellectual faculty that is the primary tool for a member of modern society. Always find ways to increase your knowledge, but more important, develop the ability to apply that knowledge to your pursuit of success.

*))) Imagination* is the one intellectual ability that is often maligned by those around us. We are told as children to stop daydreaming. As adults, we're often told to get our head out of the clouds. Yet it is the ability to dream and imagine that makes nearly everything else possible.

When you think about it (using your rational, reasoning mind), any time you set a goal to accomplish something you haven't done before, you are *imagining* your future. Without imagination, we would simply repeat previous experiences over and over. The ability to create images of things that don't yet exist lets us fly when setting goals.

Some professions, of course, promote the active use of imagination. Writers, composers, artists of all kinds—they are rewarded for their ability to use their imagination and execute what they see. Very few of us, however, earn our living in such professions. Imagination is regarded as childish and is ridiculed by those around us.

Paradoxically, everyone is looking for creative solutions to problems. So while the average person discounts the use of imagination, they appreciate its results. The ability to free your thoughts and imagine what does not yet exist is the key to success. Success is the consequence of the use of your imagination.

## Developing the intellectual faculties

Although every human being is created equal, we are not all created the same. That is, some of us have innate strengths in some areas, while others have strengths in other areas. To develop your intellectual faculties, start by analyzing your strengths and weaknesses.

For the sake of this discussion, we'll call your ability to use a particular skill *competence*. Bob Proctor calls these the four levels of competence. The first level is *unconscious incompetence*. At this level, a person is unable to exhibit particular skills or abilities, and they are also unaware that they lack the skill or ability.

People with unconscious incompetence may actually believe they are good at something, while actually being below average. (This is called the Dunning-Kruger effect, for you psychologists.) The point is that, if they were more competent, they would realize their incompetence. Don't you know of people who brag about being good drivers, even though they are actually careless, reckless, and lucky? These people are at the lowest level of knowledge when it comes to driving.

The next level of ability is called *conscious incompetence*. In this state, you are aware that you are unable to do something. It is the first real level of learning, because awareness of one's deficiencies is the first step toward competence. When you are aware that there is a gap in your knowledge or ability, you can take steps to correct it.

Next is *conscious competence*. This level is being able to do something but only with effort and concentration. If you've ever seen a child who has just learned to tie his shoes, you know the concept. When you first learn a new skill and try to put it into practice, you feel awkward as you execute the steps. Having to think about every move, every thought, results in a stilted, clumsy process.

The highest level of ability is *unconscious competence*. Abilities at this level are those you execute without having to think about it. Picture Michael Jordan as he takes a shot during a game. The body and mind know what to do so well that it happens without his being aware of it.

The levels of competence are good for estimating where you stand regarding your intellectual faculties. In some areas you will be strong, in others somewhat weaker. You have all of these capabilities already, so it's simply a matter of developing more competence in each faculty.

One habit that you can practice is that of being *in the moment*. Being in the moment means focusing on each situation as it arises, without regard to what has happened before and what will happen afterward. Every situation has an appropriate faculty associated with it. Brainstorming solutions to a problem? Imagination might be called for. Developing a flowchart for a process? Reasoning could be appropriate. Knowing how to use the appropriate application of each faculty at the proper time is a competence that will serve you well.

Being in the moment also means that you interpret the present situation on its own merits. It's been said that "Yesterday is a cancelled check; tomorrow is a promissory note. Only today is cash money." This means that to get maximum value out of a situation, you must accept it for what it is.

Proper use of the intellectual faculties means integrating them appropriately. When you think about it, imagination and memory team up well, as do perception and will. Those traits complement each other. And even though intuition and reason seem like opposites, they work well together when applied at the right times and in the right measures.

Although the intellectual faculties have been separated for discussion, they are actually all part of a recipe—the recipe for success. When used together and in the right proportions, they provide you with fantastic abilities above and beyond what you might have thought possible.

## Putting the faculties to use

Although there are many similarities in selling situations, each has its individual characteristics. I cannot instruct you in how to apply the intellectual faculties to your particular sales situation. What I can do, however, is give you a simple example of how I used them in one of my own situations—even if my use was unconscious.

Remember the sponges I talked about in the Introduction? Consider how I was able to use my intellectual faculties in my father's store. First of all, I had to use *reason* to figure out how to get rid of the sponges. We couldn't lose money on them, so my only viable option was to sell them. I used *perception* when I saw that I had access to every person who came in the store. I used *will* to make sure I mentioned sponges to every person I saw.

*Memory* enabled me to recall how my own family used sponges, while *imagination* helped me think of other ways they could be used. Finally, I used *intuition* to help me answer the question for each customer: how can this person use sponges?

I wish I could say that I was aware of what I was doing as I applied these faculties, but I wasn't. I was guided by simple desperation at having to sell a lot of sponges as quickly as possible. However, to my credit, I learned from the lesson of the sponges and applied those techniques and principles to sales from then on.

## Controlling the subconscious

All the intellectual faculties are used to control your subconscious. The subconscious is very powerful, exerting influence on everything you do. To use it effectively, you have to influence it in ways that provide you with the proper guides to your actions. Ultimately, you want to feel good about the actions that direct you toward your goals.

The process of controlling the subconscious involves using your imagination to see the possibilities and opportunities around you. Create the image of a future that fulfills your dreams and encompasses your values, and communicate that image to your subconscious.

It also involves using your memory to remember true memories, ones that support your vision of success. Focus on past successes to create a real, concrete image that you can believe in. You are a winner, and with work your subconscious mind will come to support that vision of yourself.

Question your five senses. Is what you see actually what is occurring? Or is it a false image influenced by past programming? Does your point of view affect your perception and judgment? A prudent skepticism—objectivity without negativity—can help you assess a situation quickly and accurately.

Remember that your thoughts influence your actions. If you have put in the preparatory work beforehand, the actions you take will be correct. With planning and preparation, you can focus on the positive thoughts that tell you everything possible is lined up in your favor. Filling your mind with such thoughts allows no room for negative thoughts to distract you.

## The biggest step

With all of these powers at your disposal, the biggest step you can take toward your success is to actually make the decision—the decision that you refuse to be average and ordinary. (After all, *average* is defined as "the best of the worst and the worst of the best." Who wants to be that?) The decision that you will devote yourself to achieving your goals in the various parts of your life. The decision to take control of your life and affect the situations around you rather than let them affect you.

For a salesperson, this step is momentous. You can start applying it right away, in every action you take. Once you realize that you have all of these tools available to you, you will merely need to decide which tool to use.

》》》One thought to always keep in mind: sales is an honorable profession. Your values remain part of you in every transaction, and you provide a valuable service to the world of business. Once you have made the decision that sales is your profession, you can devote your powerful intellectual faculties to being the very best.

# CHAPTER 6
## YOUR OWN WORST ENEMY

SOME MEN HAVE THOUSANDS OF
REASONS WHY THEY CANNOT DO WHAT
THEY WANT TO, WHEN ALL THEY NEED
IS ONE REASON WHY THEY CAN.

–Mary Frances Berry

Our caveman ancestor faced deadly fears on a daily basis. Basically, anything he couldn't eat would try to eat him. His fears were real and tangible. Primitive man developed a heightened sense of fear in order to survive. The human brain developed the fight or flight mechanism.

Today, we have little fear of being eaten by wild animals. Those fears have been replaced by the fear of losing our job, the fear that our significant other doesn't really love us, that we'll be late for work—a whole new spectrum of fears suited to modern society.

Comparing our current fears with what our ancestors feared, we find that most of today's fears are created by society. Do you think our ancestors suffered from paraskavedekatriaphobia, the fear of Friday the Thirteenth? Created fear or not, however, our brains are still wired like those of our ancestors, and we react to fear the same way. Our adrenaline spikes, creating a rapid heartbeat, shallow breathing, and tensing muscles.

We need to recognize fear for what it is—a message from the subconscious. Irrational or illogical fear is FEAR—false evidence appearing real—an emotion that causes a physiological response. We act upon the feeling—we move away from a scary spider or avoid the boss's office when we know we're in trouble.

Like many of the messages from the subconscious, though, fear can be triggered at the wrong time because of bad programming. Although some fears are physical and real, deserving our attention, others are imagined or simply a sign that we are moving outside our comfort zone.

Sometimes fear is bad. Intense fear can trigger the fight or flight syndrome at times when it is inappropriate to do either. We may freeze up completely, losing our ability to be effective in any way. In such cases, fear has robbed us of our resources. The word *resourceful* means "full of resources." A great definition of success is "the state of having a large number of options available." Fear takes away the options because the brain shuts down. With fewer options, we decrease our chances of taking appropriate action to counteract the source of the fear.

If this happens to you, you get in your own way—you become your own worst enemy. Your brain is less flexible and creative, and your muscles tighten, limiting your physical abilities. Dealing effectively with the problem (fight) is restricted, and so is running away (flight). Is it any wonder that we suffer from high levels of stress and anxiety, since we can't do what we're hard-wired to do?

## When fear is good

Sometimes fear is good. Feeling fear is an indication that you are taking a situation seriously. Fear of public speaking constantly ranks at or near the top of polls listing the most common fears, and even professional speakers experience nervousness before a presentation. They use the nervous energy to add excitement to their presentations. They know that if they lack at least some nervousness, their presentation will suffer from a lack of fire and passion.

This often happens to me when I give a presentation to a group. The first few sentences have that all-too-familiar feeling of fear. However, I know the fear will come, and I know it will pass. In any case, it always helps me to stay sharper than I would have been without it.

If we recognize fear as simply the way the subconscious mind tells us we're moving out of our comfort zone, we can change our perception of fear. To grow beyond our current limitations, we must do things that are uncomfortable. Remaining inside your comfort zone will limit you to the results you have received up to now. That's not growing.

A great example is the concept of resistance training in physical fitness. Most fitness experts recommend some form of resistance training—often using weights—to increase your fitness. Briefly—consult a fitness expert for full details—you lift a certain weight in a specific way a set number of times. When you can manage that task easily, you increase the weight. Your muscles become more powerful, and you become stronger.

Why do you increase the weight? Because of the body's remarkable capacity to adapt. As you lift a weight, your muscles struggle to perform the maneuver. In fact, they struggle so much that the muscle fibers actually develop minute tears. Afterward, while you are resting, the muscles repair themselves—and the fibers are stronger than they were before! *Voilà*, you are able to lift more weight.

Needless to say, it is uncomfortable to do something that literally tears your muscle fibers. Yet in doing so, you can become stronger and able to accomplish even more. You *grow*. (Note: I am by no means a physical fitness expert, so be sure to check with your doctor or certified trainer for specific lessons on what I've mentioned.)

The principle applies to all areas of your life. Your skills, confidence, and abilities will also grow when you push them to the point of discomfort. The most accomplished speakers suffer from the same fear of public speaking as everyone else, yet they continue to do it, improving with every speech as their skills increased. Fear helps them grow.

Fear can also be a motivator. Many professional athletes hate losing, to the point of actually experiencing fear. They practice relentlessly for hours so that they can avoid losing. They push themselves in big games because of their fear of losing. With preparation, practice, and performance, they become all-stars in their sport. Fear has motivated them.

## )))) How fear manifests itself

Along with the body's typical physiological reactions to fear—rapid heartbeat and shallow breathing—some people suffer from trembling, muscle weakness, and even blurred or restricted vision. Fear can become so strong that the person blacks out.

More devastating than the physical symptoms, however, are some of the behaviors that occur as fear manifests itself. As with the more subtle fears we suffer from today (compared to our ancestors), our fight or flight impulse triggers actions that are more subtle. We still try to get away from the fear but in ways that we don't always recognize.

For example, have you ever been engaged in a project or task and found yourself procrastinating? *Procrastination* is one of the killers of high performance. We may put off an unpleasant task simply because it's unpleasant, or we may delay performing a simple task because it leads to a result that triggers our fears.

Think of times that you have put off doing paperwork. Although few people enjoy filling out forms, in most businesses, it's a necessary part of the job. Putting it off may be a sign that you are experiencing some fear about completing the job. Delaying the paperwork makes no sense, especially if you depend on it to get paid, yet many people will go to great lengths to avoid it. Procrastination is fear manifesting itself.

Another sign is being prone to *distraction*. The Internet and the advent of computer use have made us, as a society, more easily distracted than ever. Fear of a particular result can nudge us into activities that have little or nothing to do with achieving our goals.

Have you ever started a task and then become absorbed in organizing your desk? Or suddenly found an interesting article in a magazine or online that you must read? You may tell yourself that things have to be in a particular order before you can move forward or that you need certain knowledge to do your job, but more often than not, such distractions are signs of your subconscious mind finding excuses for you to avoid finishing what you started.

In addition to affecting your behavior, fear affects your *mindset*. This of course influences your behavior, because your thoughts always determine your actions. When fear takes hold of you, your mind dwells on negative possibilities, reinforcing their image in your mind. This state becomes self-perpetuating, as your subconscious creates a feeling of certainty that the outcome will be negative. That certainty creates more negative images, and so on.

The negative mindset is one of the signs that fear is beginning to control you. It takes enormous will to step out of the loop of negative thinking and recognize it for what it is. Nonetheless, you must go through regular sessions of self-evaluation to correct any detours that your subconscious has forced you into. When you find yourself dwelling on negative thoughts and images, force yourself to stop. Replace them with positive images of your goals and what you hope to accomplish.

These negative aspects of fear manifest themselves when you approach the *terror barrier*. The terror barrier arises when you start something new, plan something big, or otherwise set an ambitious goal for yourself, and then become paralyzed with fear. The immensity of what you want to do overwhelms you, and you fall into fearful or negative behaviors or mindsets.

What's most insidious about the terror barrier is that it sucks the resolve right out of you. Learning how to ride a bike is scary for children, and I experienced this again recently with my grandson Aiden. More than anything in the world, Aiden wanted to ride his bike "the big boy way"—without training wheels.

After he fell over several times and endured the accompanying skinned knees and elbows, his courage began to falter. The pain and embarrassment almost beat him. Eventually, he said that he didn't *really* want to ride his bike anymore. He could walk or just ride his bike with the training wheels. The terror had trumped the importance of learning how to ride the bike.

We talked to him and encouraged him, and he got back on his bike. Of course, after a while he got the hang of it, as most children do. He quickly graduated to a bigger bike, complete with handbrakes, and now zooms all over the neighborhood.

We all encounter times when we try new things and fear locks us up. Just as with Aiden, the pain, embarrassment, angst, and feeling of being overwhelmed can make us doubt the validity of achieving our goals. We rationalize—tell ourselves "rational lies"—that the goal that's causing the pain is not worth it. Anything to avoid the pain.

In Chapter 4, I mentioned imagining goals that excite you a lot and scare you only a little. The terror barrier appears whenever the inverse happens—your fear outweighs the excitement that the goal creates. Very seldom is it because the goal is too ambitious. It happens when you lose sight of the success process.

The success process is this: any journey, task, or plan is a series of smaller steps. Each of these steps is simpler to accomplish than the project as a whole, and the smaller, more detailed the steps, the easier they become. Viewing a project as a whole, rather than as the parts that comprise it, can create fear that becomes the terror barrier.

Check the purpose of the goal that triggers the terror barrier. Occasionally, we set a goal but instinctively know that it's not the right one. I'll get more into the goal-setting process in Chapter 8, but for now I'll say that the right goal is in tune with your purpose, mission, values, and beliefs. Such a goal creates more excitement than can be trumped by fear. Analyze your goals to make sure they align with your values, and the terror barrier will have little impact on you.

## Fear of failure

Fear interferes with our success in numerous ways. One way is the *fear of failure*. The fear of failure is like the two sides of a coin. On one hand, the fear can motivate you, spurring you to work harder to accomplish your goals and to be successful. On the other hand, fear of failure can be a demotivator, completely taking the wind out of your sails.

))) Fear of failure is the result of bad programming. As has often been said, failure is only permanent if you allow it to be. Small children constantly fall down while learning to walk. They bounce right back up and try again. Sometimes they need help with their first steps, but they keep trying. If toddlers quit trying the first time they fell, no one would ever learn to walk!

The fear of failure can become overpowering, though, if our subconscious mind expects us to fail. Through negative programming, we have come to believe that we are unable to accomplish goals or to improve our lives. By giving up without trying—letting fear of failure keep us from trying—we are living down to expectations.

My daughter Tracey, who triumphed in running a marathon, went through that very experience. When she first considered running a marathon, she told me, "I could never do that." She had never been a runner before but decided she wanted to start. At first, she would run for one minute and walk for one minute. As time went on, she progressed and began to enjoy it.

Her experiences before she began to run created the doubt and fear that would prevent her from accomplishing her goal. As she progressed and began to train effectively, she broke through her fear of failure and began to focus on believing in herself more than doubting herself. Ultimately, she achieved the very thing that previously she had sworn she could "never do."

(An addendum to that story: Because of a ski injury and ensuing knee problems, I have never run a full marathon. But I ran the last 13 kilometers with Tracey during her first marathon, and her courage has enabled me to see that the full race is possible for me. I can now envision us running a marathon together.)

Fear of failure often manifests itself in language. "I'll just fail anyway" and "It's no use trying" are the messages that bad programming uses to convince us to give up. Viewed objectively, these statements are absurd. They disregard the fact that each of us is able to grow into a new role and that we can develop skills and abilities that will help us reach our goals.

For example, you might have read an article about long-distance runners and determined that you want to run a marathon. If you don't exercise regularly, carry an extra 30 pounds around your middle, and have never run a long distance, your fear of failure might stop you there, without ever seeing the possibility of success. Twenty-six miles is a long way, and your programming will tell you, "I'll never be able to do that."

The reality is that if you start small—become more active and eat more nutritiously, for example—your body will respond, and you will become more athletic. Getting instruction from other runners about running long distances might follow. After preparing properly, you arrive at the point at which running a marathon is not only possible but is simply the next step in the process. The process takes time, of course, and running a marathon is a huge athletic achievement, but thousands of people do it every year. If you overcome the fear of failure, you can join them.

## Fear of success

Oddly, many people are afflicted with the *fear of success*. Although it works more subtly, the fear of success is just as powerful as the fear of failure. The fear of success manifests itself in many ways. You might have trouble completing a project, for example. Everything has worked successfully up until close to the end, and suddenly you find yourself procrastinating (one of the signs mentioned earlier) or becoming distracted (another sign).

)))) You may find yourself sabotaging your own work. Being late for appointments, killing time, suddenly deciding on another course of action—all of these can be signs that you fear the successful completion of a project. Again, at such times you have to step outside yourself to recognize what you are doing.

Why would anyone fear success? Once more, we reflect back on bad programming. Some people fear what they might become if they are "successful." If you've been taught (and believe) that money is the root of all evil, you will have trouble succeeding at anything that will bring you substantial amounts of money. (As an aside, let me give you the complete quote: "The *love* of money is the root of all evil." Money is morally neutral.)

You may have other beliefs similar to this one. Regardless of the belief, you become the type of person you don't like only if you violate your own basic values. Programming that judges a whole class of people is destructive and can only lead to disappointment. As an individual with free will, you *choose* what kind of person you are, regardless of your accomplishments.

Others fear success because they believe that they are not up to the added responsibility or standards that success may entail. Once again, this belief disregards the ability of a human being to grow into a role. Success is not a straight line upward—there will be occasions of more success and times of less success. Quarterbacks in professional football don't complete every pass they throw. The best ones don't let incomplete passes distract them; they simply move to the next play. As you become more successful, your talents will grow also, enabling you to handle higher standards and responsibilities.

A final reason for fear of success is the perceived loss of control. We become comfortable in a given situation—that is, we maintain some sort of control over the situation. Inside the comfort zone, we are the masters of our own empire. Moving outside that zone means that there will be factors we are unfamiliar with and that may be beyond our control.

Once again, breaking a plan for success into smaller parts helps us retain some of that control. Even with such a plan, however, sometimes you simply have to trust that your preparation and hard work give you sufficient resources to handle the unexpected. Eventually, you gain more control over the new situation. The ability to trust in yourself is one way to deal with this particular fear.

Handling fear, whatever its cause, is something you have to do if you wish to be successful. Recognize it for what it is, a message that you are trying something new or different. Evaluate the fear and determine if it's real or if it's only perceived—in other words, do you need to take preemptive action to avoid a potentially bad situation? Or is it bad programming trying to assert itself in your life? Question the programming if this is the case, and eliminate it if it's adding unnecessary stress and anxiety to your life.

If you look at the new situation as an opportunity for growth, you can move from simply *handling* fear to *transforming* it. Use the fear to examine your strengths—your skills, your abilities, and the value that you add to any transaction you're involved with. Listing the resources you have available can turn a nebulous fear into a source of strength.

Because you have prepared for success, your chances for success are high. Movie star Will Smith once explained his success this way: "I will not be outworked. It's that simple. The commodity that I see in most people that aren't getting the places they want, or aren't achieving the things they want, is strictly based on hustle, on being outworked, strictly based on missing the right opportunities." Smith clearly has transformed a fear of losing into a desire to win.

## Fear and the salesperson

Salespeople suffer from the same fears as everyone else, but they have additional opportunities for self-defeating fears to affect them. These fears usually manifest themselves by interfering with the normal sales process. While more art than science, the sales process does lend itself to some analysis and categorization.

Fear often shows up in a *lack of sales activity* by the salesperson. You can't sell to customers if you aren't calling on them. If you find yourself becoming bashful or reluctant to call on customers, something has caused fear to affect you. Whether it's by phone, face to face, or some other way, by definition a salesperson has to meet and interact with people. While activity by itself does not guarantee sales success, lack of activity guarantees almost certain failure.

Fear also can show up in *diminished results*. Of course, outside factors can affect a sales environment, but if those around you are still selling, and your numbers are dropping, fear may be the reason. It may be due to the lack of activity mentioned above, or it may be because you are walking through your presentations without energy or enthusiasm. A drop in sales without some sort of explanatory factor may mean that fear is asserting itself.

One symptom that is a sure sign of fear is *negative self-talk*. You may find yourself dwelling on the negative aspects of the sales profession or on the soft spots of your product or service. Defeatist statements ("I can't sell anything"; "There's no use in trying") are self-fulfilling prophesies. Cynicism and sales do not go together.

Other signs that fear is rearing its head occur during the process itself. You may have done everything else properly and effectively, but you must do two things to be a successful salesperson: *overcome objections* and *ask for the business*.

Objections are a natural part of any sales process. Fear of objection is one of the most common fears among salespeople, but it's like a swimmer being afraid of the water. They are part of the environment you work in, and you have to handle them. The dexterity with which you handle them determines, in large part, your success as a salesperson.

First, recognize that objections will occur. It's part of human nature to resist something new. (The customer is *fearful* that he will make a bad decision.) Overcoming objections should be something that you prepare for so that when they arise, you can handle them effectively.

Objections are usually in one of three categories:

- *Generic*, having to do with sales in general

- *Product-group*, having to do with the type of product you are selling

- *Product-specific*, having to do with your particular product or service

One generic objection you can always expect, and for which you should have an answer, is, "I can't afford it." Price is an objection that every salesperson has encountered, so you should not be surprised by it. Prepare an answer for this objection, because you know it will come up. Do the same for any other anticipated objection.

The best way to counter other objections is to know your product and know your industry. Knowledge alone, however, won't overcome an objection. Remember that the customer's objection is emotional, and you have to be able to link information with emotions so that the customer can feel good about making a purchase.

Remember, the customer's purchase of your product or service is your desired result for the end of the sales process. The second way that fear can sabotage a salesperson is that, after you have gone through the process effectively, you then neglect to *ask for the business*. This last bit of timidity is fear's final attempt to sabotage your sales success. Without asking for, and getting, the business, you have not made a sale.

How do you ask for the business? First, remember that getting the sale is the whole purpose of the sales process. You can't make a sale if you don't ask. If you are nervous about this step, write a script. Depending on the situation, it can be formal, "Shall we draw up the paperwork?" or informal, "How about it?" The sales profession is too varied to include a complete list of options, but consider how you can smoothly lead into asking for the business.

As you ask for the business, concentrate on the strengths of your product or service and the benefits it will provide your customer. Finally, make sure that your request is clear—a mumbled, half-hearted attempt, diluted by self-effacing jokes, is a mark of someone who has been conquered by fear.

Fear is part of everyone's life—if they let it in. For anyone who wishes to succeed, conquering that fear and transforming it into energy they can use is the ideal way to stay on the path.

# CHAPTER 7
## The Most Valuable Tools

When a defining moment comes along, you can do one of two things. Define the moment, or let the moment define you.

–Tin Cup

# CHAPTER 7
## The Most Valuable Tools

One of the lessons I hope you got from the previous chapter is that what you focus on controls your life. Focus on negativity, and you get negative results in your life. Focus on positives and success, and you get positive results. How, then, do you go about training yourself to focus on the right things? Through questions.

Motivational author and speaker Tony Robbins often says, "The most powerful way to control your focus is through the use of questions." Moreover, the quality of your questions determines the quality of your answers. As Robbins says, "Ask lousy questions and you get lousy answers."

The power of questions comes from the process you go through to find the answers. Correctly answering deep questions requires deep thought. The most profound discoveries are made by those people who are willing to ask the right questions and then do everything they can to find the right answers.

Questions are powerful because they show that you are aware that questions must be asked. No one has all the answers. Even people we admire and want to emulate have questions. Only those who have closed their minds completely think they already know the answers. If you are serious about personal growth and success, you must first realize that life is full of questions.

Asking questions is a way to discover what you are focused on. If your main question is "Why am I such a loser?" it's safe to say that you're focused on the wrong thing. Good questions, productive questions, helpful questions, are forward-moving. Instead of "How did I get myself into this?" you might ask, "What can I do to improve the situation?" Framing the question in a way that allows progress rather than wallowing in the past helps you focus on solutions rather than problems.

Asking questions opens up possibilities. Considering the answers to high-level questions expands your thoughts to encompass options. You can ask yourself such questions as:

- What are the possibilities/possible solutions?

- If I had my choice, what would I do?

- What if I do, and what if I don't?

(See the extensive list of other powerful questions at the end of this chapter.)

On your life journey, it's especially helpful to ask questions that allow you to grow. Rephrasing bad programming as a question does not do you any good. Rewire your mind so that you can use questions to change old, unproductive programming and beliefs into something that is useful today.

As you ask questions of yourself, you may become uncomfortable with some of the answers. None of us has lived a perfect life, so we have made mistakes, developed bad habits, and have personality traits that we are ashamed of. For an honest self-appraisal, though, discovering such facets of yourself is necessary.

)) Asking yourself questions in the process of self-appraisal is crucial to moving forward. Every journey has a starting point, and you must know where you are to learn how to get where you want to be. Honesty in such a process is vital. Even if what you find out about yourself bothers you, you've made a positive move. Discovering a problem is the first step to solving it.

What kind of questions should you ask? Start with the big ones. What kind of person do you want to be? In the process of answering that question, you will confront certain truths about yourself. You will closely examine your values and beliefs. Surprises may pop up as you find people you admire that you hadn't previously considered.

What kind of life do you want to live? What do you want to be remembered for, or remembered *as*? If you knew you couldn't fail, what would you want to do most of all? Answering these questions helps you set priorities in your life.

Thinking about the possibilities that exist for you helps you decide what is important and what's not. Stop occasionally in the middle of doing something and check whether what you are doing complies with the kind of life you want for yourself. You might be surprised at how often we do things that contribute nothing to our overall goals.

What kind of people do you have around you? Are you surrounded by people who are positive and supportive? Or do you see a lot of negative faces and attitudes? Some people you have to be around because you have no choice—family members and co-workers, for instance. Their negativity affects your quality of life.

Even more important, do people around you share your dreams and aspirations? Their goals may not match yours exactly, but do they have the same passion for life? Energy feeds on itself, and when others around you are excited about the day, many more things are possible.

Another question you can ask is, "What kind of situations do I find myself in?" Often, we try to excuse our own decisions by saying that they were forced on us by the situation. For example, you might be habitually late to work because of car problems. You excuse your tardiness because of the car. Why, then, don't you do something about the car or find another way to get to work? You are in a situation of your own design. Why did you design it that way?

The big questions have been asked for ages. Philosophers since Plato and Aristotle have questioned the meaning of life. Why are we here? Are we alone? Although you may feel such questions are beyond you, they are examples of the depth of thought you must achieve if you want to live a full, enriched, successful life.

When you question the whys of your life, you are seeking the fundamentals of what your life is about. You begin to decide what is important to you and to establish priorities. Many people have spent their entire lives without ever considering what's really important. Asking these questions and *considering the answers* simplifies decisions that arise as life events happen. It doesn't matter if you don't come up with a completely satisfactory answer to each question—what matters is that you are giving thought to the subjects.

The process of self-discovery begins by asking yourself basic questions. No real growth is possible until you've taken a serious look at how you've lived your life up to now, what kind of programming you've received, how you're perceived, and whether you have obtained the results you desire.

If our lives are the results of the actions we've taken, and our actions are the results of our thoughts, then the question of how you've lived your life reflects your thought processes up to now. Although no one is perfect or lives the perfect life, are you happy overall with how you've lived? Don't dwell on the negatives in your life, but give them some consideration. What decisions have you made that you would make differently now?

I've talked previously about how programming affects you. Taking time to examine what has influenced you in the past is a productive exercise that can liberate you. By recognizing and realizing influences, you can judge them to decide whether they are worth keeping or whether you need to reject them.

It's common wisdom that you shouldn't live your life according to the expectations of others. However, the way other people perceive you can reveal your blind spots. What we see in the mirror is always affected by our own biases and prejudices. Considering, or even asking, how other people see us can be an enlightening experience.

A useful tool for self-discovery and perception is the *Johari window*. The Johari window is an exercise in which you and people who know you select adjectives from a list to describe you. You would choose five or six adjectives to describe yourself. Your peers independently choose five or six they think describe you. The results are then mapped in a grid of four quadrants.

The descriptors fall into four categories. Those words that both you and your peers used fall into the category *Arena*—traits known to yourself and also to others. The Arena reflects characteristics that represent you accurately to the world.

Words that you chose but few or none of your peers chose are considered your *Façade*. This reflects things that you know—or think you know— about yourself but that others don't perceive about you.

Characteristics that others choose but you didn't go into the category known as *Blind Spots*. This is one of the most enlightening categories, because you may be surprised at how others perceive you.

The category *Unknown* includes the words that neither you nor your peers used to describe you. These adjectives my not have been used because they don't apply, or because both you and the others are ignorant of them in your behaviors.

The Johari window is not the only tool available for self-discovery, but it can be very helpful in letting you see how others perceive you. Match this against how you want others to perceive you, and how transparent your behavior is in reflecting your true personality. Aligning your actions with your values reflects both a confidence and a maturity that help you succeed.

When you examine your life, have you achieved the results you desired? Without being judgmental, analyze your life and see if you have compromised more often than you have achieved what you wanted. Have you settled for less, or have your results exceeded your expectations? Your results are the one true measure of how well your purpose, vision, and mission align.

Answering these questions helps you answer the one big question: *What kind of person am I?* Your actions and the perceptions of other people provide the only real answer to this question. If you mull over this question, you are on the road to true self-awareness. Answering it honestly can lead to some hard realizations about yourself. Every person aspires to be more than he is, but ultimately you have to be able to like yourself. If you have become someone you don't like, you probably have already felt that as you look in the mirror. The subconscious mind answered the question long ago.

The good news is that you can begin today, right now, to correct that self-perception. You can become someone you're happy to be, someone other people enjoy being around. Your actions determine your life, and a single step can put you on the path to success in all areas.

Think about it. If you are driving to a destination and suddenly determine that you are on the wrong road, you don't continue in the same direction, filled with self-loathing because you're not going where you want to go. You figure out how to get back on the right road, make a turn (and some turns are sharper than others), and continue your trip going in the right direction. Deciding to get on the right road is something you can do *now*.

## Values

Albert Einstein said, "Try not to become a person of success, but rather try to become a person of value."

When answering the question about what kind of person you want to be, you are enumerating your *values*. I've talked quite a bit about values previously, but during the phase when you ask yourself questions, an analysis of your values is absolutely vital. They determine and reflect your beliefs, your programming, and everything you are as a person.

Your values guide your actions. Most people never make a conscious study of their values, so they are never completely sold on them. Values they think are important become flexible, candidates for sacrifice if a situation becomes too difficult or causes them anxiety and pain. They know that they are compromising themselves because of a temporary condition.

There are many times in life when it pays to be flexible, pliant, and compromising. Your values, however, should never be compromised— not if you want to achieve peace of mind and true, lasting success. Doing the right thing—adhering to your values, in other words—is enormously difficult sometimes. The person who acts in accordance with values, however, enjoys serenity and the respect of other people. Temporary discomfort is a small price to pay for such valuable gains.

》 For the professional salesperson, knowing your own values helps you evaluate your customers' values. Why is that important? Because if you emphasize areas in which your values are in alignment with theirs, you achieve an affinity that is very powerful.

For example, *honesty* is a basic value that is shared by most people. Even in a time when everyone is being careful with their money, don't you know of businesspeople who charge more than their competition, yet are successful because of their reputation for honesty? These successful people have likely occasionally sacrificed temporary financial gain to best serve their customers. For example, an honest person might tell the customer, "Product A is more expensive than Product B, but B works just as well as A."

Knowing your customers' values not only helps you develop a better relationship with them, but it also prevents you from misreading a cue and trying to align yourself with the wrong value. For example, a customer may want to start gossiping about a competitor. If spreading or engaging in rumors is against your values ("Respect for those who are not present to defend themselves"), you wouldn't participate.

The customer who, in a moment of weakness, violates one of his own values recognizes what he has done. He will respect you for helping him get back on track. If the customer lacks that particular value, you have at least earned his respect for staying true to your own. Even those who don't adhere to values admire those who do.

## )) Purpose

Closely related to your values is your *purpose*. Most people drift through life without a purpose, merely responding to whatever winds life blows their way. When you know your purpose, however, you have a direction, something that helps you adjust your sails so that, regardless of how the wind blows, you move closer to your destination.

We are all put on this planet for a reason. Although born equal, we are not born the same. Some people have an artistic bent, whereas others are good with numbers. Many are blessed with mechanical ability, others with tremendous athletic potential.

Think about the times in your life that you have felt most in sync with what was happening. It's almost as though a tuning fork had been struck and touched to your soul. Maybe you happily created pottery from raw clay. Perhaps it was when you helped another person resolve a problem that was beyond him. You might have felt this way when teaching a skill or a piece of knowledge to a group.

The particular experience could have been anything. It happened when you touched upon your purpose, your own reason for being. It was the answer to the question raised previously: why am I here? The answer to that question is your *purpose*.

Once you know your real purpose, you can focus your *vision* on fulfilling that purpose. Your vision is the image you create that embodies what you think is your potential. If your purpose is to be an artist, you might have a vision of your paintings hanging on the walls of a museum. If your purpose is to be a teacher, you might see yourself in front a classroom full of children, a university class, or a business class of employees.

You can see why knowing your purpose has to come before creating your vision. If you feel most fulfilled when working on a car's engine, for example, a vision of being a teacher would merely create conflict in your mind. Even if you achieved your vision, you would still be missing that spark that tells you you're doing the right thing.

Visions are often influenced by those around us who impose their programming on us. By knowing your purpose and then creating a vivid, concrete image of yourself engaged in your purpose, you focus your subconscious mind on what you really want to achieve in life. You create your own programming.

After you have created your vision, you articulate it through a *mission*. Whereas the vision is simply an image, your mission uses language to describe your path toward making that vision real. The vision engages the subconscious mind, and the mission engages the conscious mind.

When you were a child, at some point someone probably asked you what you wanted to be when you grew up. Your answer, even as a child, was a mission. True, it lacked the substance of true consideration, experience, judgment, and maturity, but it articulated a plan for the future.

Your mission will be your strategy for creating your vision. You don't have specifics, but you know the general direction you have to go. Mission is like a compass. The compass keeps you on course as you travel. You may encounter hills, valleys, canyons, and vast stretches without landmarks, but the compass keeps you true.

The mission may be something like, "I want to be a marine biologist." You realize that you will need specialized training, and that mental and physical fitness are required. Perhaps your mission is to be a web designer or an astronaut (with new technology, an increasingly available choice for many people). You know that you will need to fulfill particular requirements for any of these missions.

At this point you don't have details; those will come later, as you set goals (which I'll discuss in the next chapter). What you do have, however, is a framework within which you can set goals that are attuned with the more fundamental phases—your purpose, your values, and your vision. Mission is a strategy for achieving success.

That last statement is key, regardless of what position you're in, or how long you intend to stay there. We all have taken positions that are a temporary part of our lives, in situations that are transitional. You may be in sales or some other job, not as a career but for the moment, because you're going to school, because it's the only job available, or because it's a step toward the position you ultimately seek.

Regardless of how long you intend to stay in your position, you will learn and achieve much more if you view it through the prism of purpose, values, vision, and mission. By doing so, you practice the skills you'll need when you reach the position you're looking for. At the same time, you will accomplish and achieve much more at your current level or position.

In other words, bringing your full powers to whatever stage of your career you are currently in, whether transitional or permanent, will help you develop the habit of excellence in all you do. That is the one habit you want to practice every chance you get.

This chapter has focused extensively on self-discovery and introspection. The ancient Greek aphorism "Know thyself" stands as timeless advice. Regardless of the field you choose, having knowledge of who you are at your very core will add confidence and credibility to your actions.

For the professional salesperson, building on a foundation of self-awareness and alignment with your own values makes the sales process easier. You are engaged in a profession that civilization depends on. Without salespeople, goods would stay in storage, forever unsold. By having the confidence to interact with customers on that level—because you know who you are and what you're doing—you will light the spark that enables you to be successful.

## SAMPLE POWER QUESTIONS

- What do you think is best?
- How do you feel about it?
- What led up to _____?
- What have you tried so far?
- What seems to confuse you?
- Then what?
- How does this fit with your plans/values/way of life?
- What are the other angles you can think of?
- What is just one more possibility?
- Like what? Such as?
- What other ideas do you have about it?
- What if it doesn't work out the way you wish?
- What if this doesn't work?
- And if this fails what will you do?
- How do you want it to be?
- If you could do it over again, what would you do differently?
- If it were you, what would you have done?
- How else could a person handle this?
- If you could do anything you wanted, what would you do?
- What seems to be the main obstacle?
- What is stopping you?

- What concerns you the most about _____?
- What will you have to do to get the job done?
- What support do you need to accomplish _____?
- By when will you do it?
- What information do you need before you decide?
- What do you know about it now?
- How do you suppose you can find out more about it now?
- What was the lesson/learning?
- What was your part in this?
- What were you responsible for?
- If you had free choice in the matter/wiped the slate clean, what would you do?
- If the same situation came up again, what would you do?
- In the bigger scheme of things, how important is this?
- What is your game plan about it?
- What kind of plan do you need to create?
- How do you suppose you could improve the situation?
- What are the chances of success?
- If you do this, how will it affect _____?
- How does this affect the whole picture?
- What else do you need to take into consideration?
- What action will you take? And after that?
- What are your next steps?

# CHAPTER 8
## GOAL SETTING AND GOAL GETTING

THERE IS A DIFFERENCE.....BETWEEN
INTEREST AND COMMITMENT. WHEN
YOU'RE INTERESTED IN DOING
SOMETHING, YOU DO IT ONLY WHEN
IT'S CONVENIENT. WHEN YOU'RE
COMMITTED TO SOMETHING, YOU
ACCEPT NO EXCUSES, ONLY RESULTS.

–Kenneth Blanchard

# CHAPTER 8
## GOAL SETTING AND GOAL GETTING

Near my home is a hiking trail that goes up Grouse Mountain, at the top of which is a small collection of shops and restaurants, along with a ski chalet. There are two ways to get to the top: ride a gondola or hike the trail. The hiking trail is very steep—it's unofficially known as "Mother Nature's Stairmaster." When I take friends there, we usually ride the gondola to the top. (Most of my friends refuse to believe that there is a trail. As far as they're concerned, the gondola's the only way.) When I'm alone, I often hike that trail, sometimes for pleasure and other times to see how quickly I can do it. My competitive nature comes out when I do this for exercise.

Before I begin each hike, I decide what my *goal* is for that day—pleasure or competition. If it's pleasure, I take it leisurely, enjoying nature and the pleasantness of the experience. If my goal is competition, I pace myself aggressively, concentrating only on moving one foot in front of the other as smoothly as possible.

Because I set a goal beforehand, I'm able to take advantage of my purpose for that hike. It would be silly to say I'm doing it for pleasure, then speed up the hill with my head down, concentrating on my feet. Both the experience and my efforts would be wasted.

In the same way, goal setting is a way for you to progress toward your success one step at a time. By determining your goal ahead of time, and then moving along the trail you've outlined for yourself, you eventually reach the top. Setting and attaining goals is the process by which the rubber meets the road (or in my case, where the hiking boot meets the dirt): the fulfillment of your purpose, your mission, and your vision.

The rest of the process outlined in the previous chapter amounts to nothing more than a wish if you don't set goals. Someone occasionally stumbles upon an opportunity that helps them move closer to realizing their vision, but doing that is trusting your future to chance. Gambling on the future makes people lethargic and apathetic. They turn over control of their destiny to the whims of fate. Successful people don't do that—they take matters into their own hands.

As I discuss goals and goal setting in this chapter, remember that setting effective goals is a skill that must be developed. The more you do it, the better you'll get at it. What I present here is information that can shorten your learning curve so that you will be able to achieve your dreams more quickly.

What is a goal? It's a *plan* for taking the steps necessary to create your vision of success in concrete form. If you've established a mission that is in line with your purpose and your values, you have gone a long way toward establishing a good goal. Whereas the mission is a broad outline of where you want to go, a goal is the detailed line that takes you from point A to point B and beyond.

One of the greatest accomplishments in adventuring is climbing Mount Everest, the highest peak in the world. To reach the summit takes months or even years of planning and preparation. The top of the mountain is so high that it takes several days to reach. For that reason, various camps have been established along the way.

Expert climbers don't simply start climbing and continue until they reach the top. They formulate a plan that involves first reaching one camp, then reaching the next, and so on. Their plans must be flexible as they adapt their routes to accommodate weather, ice conditions, or anything else that comes along. They conquer Everest in small bites, not in one gulp.

One analogy that many people find useful is to think of the goal-setting process as making a *map*. You know where you are, and you know where you want to go. Your goals are the locations in between the two through which you must pass to reach the final destination. Sometimes the journey is a straight path, but often it zigzags as new situations present themselves. Intermediate steps must be met so you can go the next location.

As with maps of physical locations, there are usually many ways to get to a specific place. What you are doing with your goals is choosing one way among many options, the way that is best for you. Other people may choose other goals and other routes to success. That's what makes us individuals. At the same time, you may find travelers who can move along with you for a distance, making the journey more pleasant. Ultimately, however, your map is designed for you alone, because only you can make the trip for yourself.

Your goal setting also helps you *focus* on what you need to do. Earlier, I discussed the multiple distractions that can interfere with your journey. By knowing exactly what you need to do next to move closer to your goal, you can disregard the shiny things and butterflies that flutter across your field of vision. Although it's tempting to follow something that seems attractive on the surface, you know that the next step is your guide to actual success.

In that way, even though having goals frees your mind from many other concerns, your thoughts are actually *anchored* to an effective process. An anchored boat resists the waves that can push it around and drive it off course. The big difference, of course, is that even though your thoughts are anchored, you—unlike an anchored boat—are moving.

There are a few very important factors to consider when it comes to setting goals. First, you have to *take your goals seriously*. Although you can have goals in a variety of areas of your life, unless you are committed to following through on the process and reaching your goal, setting the goal does little good.

The previous paragraph touches on something important. Some of your goals will be life-changing, creating a new reality for yourself and possibly even your family. These are immense goals that may take years to accomplish. Other goals will be much lighter in nature. For example, you may have a goal to learn a new language simply for the pleasure of doing it. These goals are set the same way as weightier goals.

In this way, your goals are very *personalized to you*. In the example, you may want to learn a new language because it will open your mind to a different culture, or you may be planning a trip to a foreign country in which that language is spoken. In either case, if the goal is important to you, it has validity.

Remember that I said goal setting is like a map, where there are different routes to the same destination? Beware of advice from others who have similar goals but choose a different route. The route they have chosen may be right for them but not for you. Your process is yours alone. Although it may not match someone else's process, as long as it's effective, you can rest assured that it's the best plan for you.

⟩⟩ It's important also that any goals you set align with your *values*. You may be tempted to take a shortcut, but unless it's part of your value system, it's doomed before you even start. Many people have the goal of making a lot of money. Some people play the lottery with that in mind; others rob banks. It almost goes without saying—*almost*—that methods such as the latter violate all kinds of values for most people.

Another important aspect of goal setting is that you have to *know what you want*. I'll go into more detail later about specificity in setting goals, but this deals with the bigger issue of knowing your purpose. Goal setting must be preceded by the preparatory work described in the previous chapter. Without knowing your true purpose, you will lack the real commitment and seriousness necessary to achieve your goals.

Life is full of wants—you *want* to lose weight, you *want* to have more money, you *want* to have better relationships—but most of our desires don't fit in with our true purpose in life. Frivolous, momentary desires are part of the human condition. They are the distractions that can deceive you if you let them.

Finally, the process of setting goals is creating a plan of *action*. Many people create outlines for books that never get written, or draw sketches for paintings that are never put to canvas. Setting goals without a commitment to do what is necessary to achieve them is just another exercise in futility. Even worse, it can fool you into believing that you are making progress when all you are doing is finding a way to avoid taking action. Create your goals with the idea firmly in mind that this is something that you are going to *do*.

## Staying on track

One of the key benefits of goal setting is helping you fight off the negative emotions that have held you back up to now. Bad programming always tries to reassert itself. It is a battle, especially when just starting out, to keep that programming from taking control of your subconscious and preventing your success.

Fear and uncertainty are almost sure to pop up occasionally as you begin working toward your success. Treat them as old acquaintances that you no longer want around. Focus on your goals and the steps you are taking to be successful, and their power over you will fade.

Since goal setting is the simple process of following one step after another to create the life you want for yourself, your vision will become more real to you, more concrete. Instead of negative emotions that hold you back, you will start to think, *I can do this!* That thought alone—the realization that success is possible—will do more to fight off negativity than anything else.

On a more mundane level, planning and preparatory work maximize your chances for real success. When you take the goal setting process seriously, you analyze the steps to make sure that they are practical. You leave little to chance when you set goals. The plan you create may not be the quickest, objectively speaking, but it's the best for you.

When a mechanic works on your engine, he verifies that all the parts are working. Based on his training and experience, he knows to look for certain problems. If a part needs to be replaced, he checks to see if it's available. He doesn't take the engine apart and then wait for the part to magically appear.

Like the mechanic, you apply your own experience and training to setting your goals. You know what you need to achieve a particular step, and you act accordingly. It's a straightforward process that makes success nearly inevitable. There is no mystery or magic involved—you are working toward your goal.

Finally, since you have each step of your climb to success mapped out, you can fight being overwhelmed, by focusing completely on the step that is in front of you. You can use your plan to block out the factors that have previously intimidated you. You're not taking a giant leap to achieve this HUGE SUCCESS; you are simply taking a small step.

## ))))) Components of an effective goal

How do you go about designing your goals so that they are most effective? Although different people have their own ways of setting goals, most goals have several characteristics in common. Their goals are specific, have a time frame, are achievable through their own efforts, are measurable, and address priorities. You can use the acronym STAMP to help remember these characteristics as you design your own goals.

*Specific.* The human mind is a tremendous instrument, but it does have one limitation—it can think about only one thing at a time. With this in mind, you want to set a goal that achieves a single purpose. You might want to lose weight and increase your wealth, and both of those are worthwhile goals. However, they are two *separate* goals.

Since one of the benefits of goal setting is to focus your efforts, it makes sense to emphasize that focus by concentrating your goal setting on only one goal at a time. Being specific means addressing only one issue at a time with your goals. Want to lose weight? Fine, write it down as a goal. Increase your net worth? Write it down as another goal. Learn a language? Do the same.

*Time frame*. People who set goals without a time frame in which to accomplish them are guilty of the "somedays." You've heard it before: "*Someday*, I'm going to lose weight" or "*Someday*, I'll write that novel I've been meaning to write." Those who depend on such statements are not serious about achieving their goal. It's simply a wish.

Setting a deadline to achieve your goal also creates a sense of urgency. As soon as you establish a time frame, the clock is ticking. You create pressure on yourself to get things done. This urgency is a sign that you take success seriously. A partial example of setting a goal using the criteria we've learned so far is, "I'm going to lose 30 pounds [specific] within six months [time frame]." One way to set a goal is to use the *WOW* formula. What can you accomplish *within one week*?

*Achievable*. I've talked at various points about taking control of your life. When you make your goal achievable, you establish that it is something you can affect through your own efforts. Some goals may involve working with other people, but good goals never leave anything to chance. "Winning the lottery" is not a goal, because it's not something you can achieve without fate falling your way.

*Measurable*. Because you are engaging in actions to reach your goal, it helps to have milestones along the way to mark your progress. For example, if your goal is to increase your sales by $1,000 per week, you can break it down so that you can measure your progress. Let's say that you earn a $200 commission on each sale, and that you average one sale for every three presentations you make to your customers. To earn $1,000 more per week, you will have to see 15 more customers each week, an average of 3 more per day.

That kind of increase may stretch your abilities at first. You may struggle to add even one more customer each day. Do that, though, and you will earn an extra $1,000 every three weeks—not quite at the level to which you aspire, but progress nonetheless. That progress is what you can see when your goal is measurable.

*Priority*. Finally, you want to *prioritize* your goals. We've established that you can have different goals for different areas of your life and the different roles you lead. Because we each have limited time, you may occasionally have to choose between two goals. Knowing in advance what's important helps you organize your time so that you work on those items that move you closer to success.

This choice, which we'll address later, is one of the key factors in success. A goal at one time may be more important, and at another time, less important. For example, you understand that to achieve more professionally, you occasionally have to sacrifice time with your family. At certain times, however, work must take a back seat so that you can focus on your relationships. Always keep your priorities in mind. Remember the acronym WIN. Ask yourself, "What's important now?"

Why is it important to know what you want when establishing your goals? Because we often work hard at achieving success in a particular area, only to find that it wasn't what we wanted at all. The majority of people fall into their professions and lifestyles by accident or by circumstance. They reach retirement age and realize how empty life was for them.

Stephen R. Covey describes this situation as climbing the ladder of success, only to discover that the ladder was leaning against the wrong wall. There are many unfortunate people who find themselves in the middle of a career that goes against their values, while ignoring what they should have been doing all along—that is, their purpose. Knowing what you want is one of the key steps in establishing worthwhile goals.

Goal setting involves activities. This is because *progress is movement*. All the words we use to describe progress portray action—climbing the ladder, walking the path, leaping to the next level. Instinctively, we understand that success is not achieved by contemplating your navel. Aligning your goals so that you are engaged in activity while reaching them works with your nature rather than against it.

As you engage in the activity called for in achieving your goal, you can take the opportunity to evaluate your goal. Does what you're doing seem effective? Does it feel productive? Are you achieving results? Evaluating your progress through activity is the only way to really know if you are making progress. It helps if you use a shorthand tool to measure your goals, constantly ask yourself, "How much, by when?"

Evaluating your plan is important because you are engaged in real life. Every plan is perfect in theory. Only when it has withstood the flame of real life can you determine whether it is going to work or not. Experienced football coaches know this. They design their plays to take advantage of their team's strengths. On paper, the Xs and Os work perfectly every time.

Only when the plays are put into action against another team, however, can their effectiveness be determined. The playbook is often revised on the fly as opposing forces work to thwart the plays. It's the same way with your goals. Only activity in the real world can prove a plan worthy or not.

Through activity, you increase your skills. As you engage in the work necessary to achieve your goals, you may occasionally find areas in which you lack skills. By continuing your activities, you become more adept and able. The number and level of your skills increase, part of the adaptive process I mentioned earlier. You are able to do more because you are doing more.

### The law of reciprocity

)))  One principle that you must keep in mind when setting goals is this: what are you willing to give in return for reaching your goal? There is nothing mysterious about this condition. If you want to become physically fit, you might give up desserts or an hour of sleep in the morning so you can exercise before work.

It's a rule of the universe that there's no such thing as a free lunch. This rule, the Law of Reciprocity, is simply a factor that must be obeyed, just as we obey the law of gravity. If you want to receive from the universe, you must give something back to the universe.

Recognizing this law helps avoid the something-for-nothing mentality that afflicts so many people. They believe that they should receive all kinds of rewards even though they contribute nothing to the world. Expecting rewards without a corresponding payment is immature and unrealistic. There is a price to be paid for success. The question is, are you willing to pay it? You have to know the answer to that question beforehand.

Being a taker all the time also creates a passivity that can squash success. If you are only interested in what's in it for you, you give control to the universe or to other people. When you work hard and give back to the world, you are engaged in an activity that naturally carries with it rewards.

Once you have established your goals, write them down. Putting your goals down in concrete form engages your language-using conscious mind and allows you to use your intellectual faculties to make the goals real. The written statement is an act of commitment and a reminder to you that you are serious about your goals.

In written form, your goal should:

- Follow the STAMP formula

- Be written in the present tense as though it has already happened

$\rangle\rangle\rangle$ By writing and articulating your goal in the present tense, you will experience a sensation more closely connected to what you want to feel. This sensation is in tune with how you'll feel when you reach your goal. Experience that feeling of achievement now and let yourself enjoy it throughout your goal-getting process. The vibrations I spoke of earlier will kick up to this "achieved" sensation, and you'll be in the right attraction vibration.

Read your goals aloud twice a day, first thing in the morning and before you go to bed at night. This engages more of your senses, establishing the reality of what you are doing. *Expect* the goal to be achieved. You have to believe in it and expect that you will get it; otherwise, the goal is not effective, and you are wasting time setting it. Using the STAMP formula will help, but you have to be a true believer in the achievement of the goal.

Finally, get started on your goals *now*. Ready or not, work on your goals. The truth is, there is no perfect time to set your goals, and waiting for the perfect time will immobilize you. Get things almost right and jump in. Adjust your plan if you need to, but get started right away.

Don't confuse planning with doing, and don't expect perfection from yourself. Your ability to create and execute your plans is a skill that will develop over time. Do the best you can every step of the way, and you are well on the way to goal-setting success.

# CHAPTER 9
## LEAPING INTO ACTION

YOU HAVE BRAINS IN YOUR HEAD
AND FEET IN YOUR SHOES. YOU CAN
STEER YOURSELF ANY DIRECTION
YOU CHOOSE. YOU'RE ON YOUR OWN
AND YOU KNOW WHAT YOU KNOW,
AND YOU ARE THE ONLY ONE WHO'LL
DECIDE WHERE TO GO.

–Dr. Seuss

# CHAPTER 9
## LEAPING INTO ACTION

The discussion of time is so important that I've given it its own chapter. Ultimately, all you have is time and what you do with it. All of the exercises, strategies, ideas, and so on are worthless unless and until you put them into action. If you spend your time doing things other than what will propel you toward your goals, you are cheating yourself.

Time is the only resource that all of us have in equal proportion. Those who seem to have more of it simply get more done in the same amount of time. You never "get" more time, for example, to make sales calls on customers. How you choose to spend your time defines who you are and what kind of life you have chosen to live.

)) There's no such thing as time management. There is only *self-management* and managing the activities to which you devote your time. *Activities management* is the key. Until someone invents a time machine, there is no way to stop time or dam it up to stop its flow or put it away to be used later. Time cannot be managed.

On the other hand, you can manage yourself quite well. You can choose to squander the 1,440 minutes you have each day, or you can squeeze each one to get the absolute most out of it. So although you will see the phrase *time management* tossed around, don't be fooled—nobody bosses time around.

Time is about choices. Some experts say that you can achieve physical fitness in as little as 30 minutes a day. Spend an hour a day writing one page of your novel, and you can finish in a year. Authors who write a novel every year, year in and year out, are considered quite prolific. Want a clean house? Spend 15 minutes a day cleaning, and you'll work wonders. Want to learn a new language? Spend an hour a day studying, and in a year you'll be fluent.

Get the idea? When you consistently choose to work on specific projects that are goal-related, you can achieve more than you ever thought possible.

# PHILOSOPHY 101

Once, a philosophy professor stood before his class with some items in front of him. When the class began, he picked up a large empty jar and began to fill it with rocks about the size of his fist. When no more rocks would fit, he asked the class, "Is the jar full?" They agreed that it was.

The professor picked up a box of pebbles and poured them into the jar. He lightly shook it, and the pebbles rolled into the spaces between the rocks. When the pebbles reached the top of the jar, he asked the class again, "Is the jar full?" They laughed and answered yes.

Finally the professor picked up a box of sand and poured it into the jar. It filtered into every small space available. He poured quite a bit of sand into the jar until it reached the top. He shook the jar until it all settled.

**"Now,"** he said, **"I want you to recognize that this is your life.** The rocks are the important things—your family, your partner, your health, your children, all the things that, if everything else were lost and only they remained, your life would still be full. The pebbles are the other things that matter, like your job, your house, your car. The sand is everything else, the small stuff.

**"If you put the sand into the jar first, you don't have room for the pebbles or the rocks.** The same goes for your life. If you spend all your time and energy on the small stuff, you will never have time for the things that are important to you. Pay attention to the things that are critical to your happiness. Play with your children. Take time to get medical checkups.

Take your partner out dancing. There will always be time to go to work, clean the house, give a dinner party, and fix the disposal.

**"Take care of the rocks first**—the things that really matter. Set your priorities. The rest is just sand."

Think about all the time-wasters you indulge in. How much time do you spend watching television? According to a 2006 survey by the Bureau of Labor and Statistics, Americans spend an average of 2.6 hours a day watching television. That's about the same amount of time it would take for you to be physically fit, write a novel, learn a language, and have a clean house.

*Choices.*

# THE SEVEN NATURAL LAWS OF THE UNIVERSE

Laws exist all around us. We are mostly aware of the manmade laws that control our behavior and society. Other laws, however, are more powerful and demanding. We cannot violate these laws, just as we can't violate the law of gravity. They are the laws of nature and the universe, and we absolutely must heed them. I won't go into much detail on these laws, and the definitions below are extremely brief representations of what they really are. (For more information on the universal laws and how they affect our lives, I recommend the works of Bob Proctor, Wallace D. Wattles, and Mary Morrissey, among others.) Your life will be much more productive, satisfying, and successful if you keep these laws in mind as you make decisions.

)) *Law of Perpetual Transmutation*: Energy always moves into a physical form. For example, when you make a decision (a thought, a form of energy), it translates into action (an expression of that thought in the physical world). A mental image becomes a solid object in the physical world.

)) *Law of Vibration*: Everything in the universe is in a constant state of motion at a given frequency. It's as though each of us is a radio tuned to a particular station. When the world around us or other people are tuned to the same station—are on the same frequency or state of vibration—there is harmony. When we are tuned to different stations, everything is more difficult or just out of sync. (The Law of Attraction is a subset of the Law of Vibration.)

)) *Law of Gender/Gestation*: Everything starts as a seed, or a beginning stage of growth. Our personal development—or a new idea—works the same way. We plant these seeds today for what we will reap when the time is right. As Ecclesiastes says, "To everything there is a season."

)) *Law of Relativity*: Nothing is large or small, good or bad, rich or poor, unless you have something to contrast it with. Relationships are the key to this law. Our perspective affects our judgment.

)) *Law of Opposites/Polarity*: For everything in the universe, there is an opposite. For every down, there is an up; for every dark, a light; for every negative, a positive. In the same way, for every reason you *can't* do something, there is a reason you *can* do it.

)) *Law of Rhythm*: Just as day follows night and the high tide follows the low, our lives are guided by the rhythms of the universe. Everything moves in cycles. Recognize and work with the rhythms and take advantage of them. For example, during a downturn in the business cycle, use the lessons you learn to prosper even more when business picks up—and it always will.

)) *Law of Cause and Effect*: This is the law that many of us are aware of but that we try to ignore. For every action, there is a reaction. Negative examples of this law abound. If we overspend, we become broke. If we eat too much, we become fat. On the other hand, if we study hard, we learn more. If we work hard, we become wealthier and build inner strength. The essence of the law is that whatever we send out into the universe comes back to us. (The Law of Reciprocity is a subset of this law.)

Other laws also exist, but they are refinements of these laws. These seven laws command and control our lives. Ignore them, and you will suffer from constant disappointment and frustration. Embrace these universal laws, and you will prosper.

The tools, techniques, and ideas that follow have been tested and tried for hundreds of years, so you can have faith in them. All of them may not suit your temperament right now, and that's okay. Take what works for you and use it. At a later time, if you decide to try some of the rest, they'll still be there.

## Avoid crises

One of the biggest time-wasters is having a crisis mentality. When things go wrong, all your other planning goes out the window until you take care of the urgent problem that jumps in your face. Handling small problems before they escalate into big problems can save you more time than almost anything else.

Stephen R. Covey discusses activities as being in four quadrants. (He first mentioned the quadrants in *The 7 Habits of Highly Effective People*, and then expanded on the concept in *First Things First*, coauthored with A. Roger and Rebecca R. Merrill.) Some activities are *Important*, and some are *Urgent*. Other activities are both *Important* and *Urgent*, and others are neither. I won't ruin the books for you by going into more detail, but essentially Covey says that activities that are *Important*, but not *Urgent*, are the ones that prevent emergencies and crises. That means looking at areas in your life where you seem to have crises more often and analyzing those areas to determine the cause or causes. Then plan your actions ahead of time to avoid the crises.

A friend of mine once heard a whining noise coming from somewhere in the back of his car. A terrible burning smell occurred at the same time. A mechanic looked at it and said that there was a problem with the drive train. He could patch it up fairly cheaply so the car would keep running, but he couldn't guarantee how long his patch job would last. To get it fixed right would cost several hundred dollars more.

Understand, there would be no noticeable improvement in the car's performance, handling, gas mileage, or anything else. It would simply continue to run as it was supposed to do. My friend scheduled an appointment with the mechanic the next day and got the car fixed. Soon he was driving the car just as he always had, except without the noise and the smell.

My friend could have saved the money by driving the car until it broke down, but then the repairs would have been done in a crisis. He would have had to take time off work to deal with the emergency, along with all the emotional turmoil it would cause. By getting the repairs done on his own schedule, my friend avoided being stranded on the side of the road.

Select the problem that seems to crop up most often. Figure out what you need to determine the cause of that problem, and schedule time every day to eliminate the cause. You'll be amazed at the time you save because of what *doesn't* happen.

## Budget time

Imagine you were given $500 a day to spend any way you wish. Out of that money, you'd have to pay for all your living needs, such as housing, food, clothing, utilities, and so on. The only stipulation was that, at the end of each day, whatever money you had left would vanish, and the next day you would start out at zero.

Most of us would feel very prosperous with that amount of money. What would happen, though, if you spent all the money you received on trivial items? You could still wind up on the last day of the month without enough money to take care of your needs.

)) Each minute of every day is as precious as those dollars. Working on a time budget involves two things: *evaluation* and *planning*. You can squander your time, or you can invest it. Squandering time is like throwing money in the trash. You get no real value from it, and it could have been spent on something more important.

The problem with evaluating how you spend your time is that the same activity can be either an investment or a waste, depending on when it's done, the reason it's done, and the result of doing it.

No one would argue that sleeping every day is wasted time. But if you're sleeping excessively long periods to avoid having to do anything else, you're wasting time. If you feel suddenly sleepy whenever you have a difficult task ahead of you, sleeping would be a waste. If you're napping during the day when you should be meeting with other people, it's a waste.

Television can be one of the biggest time-wasters, or it can be a great way to educate yourself. Carefully selecting the programs you watch, rather than channel surfing until you find something, turns a time-waster into a planned source of entertainment.

I hope that I haven't given you the impression that every moment of every day you should be working. Entertainment is important. Rest is important. We all need to spend time renewing our energy, physically, mentally, and emotionally. Reading a book, exercising, and even watching television can revitalize your life so that when you are working, you get more accomplished and more satisfaction from what you do.

Keep a *time log* for a couple of days to see how much time you spend on various activities throughout your day. Be honest, and don't be judgmental—yet. Write down what you do and how much time you spend doing it, providing just a bare record of the information.

After you have a few days recorded, look at each activity and evaluate it. Is it something you really wanted to do? Is it important to you? If you spend an hour a day visiting with your friends, was the entire hour valuable, or would 30 minutes have been just as valuable? You're the only one who can determine the value of each activity.

Activities such as visiting with friends or watching television can function as times of renewal, recharging your batteries as you enjoy yourself. Most of us are not in the position of "all work and no play"; if anything, most of us quit too soon without working hard enough to achieve our goals.

But there is the story of the two lumberjacks. (My fellow tree-huggers, don't get hung up on lumberjacks. I need them to make my point.) They are having a contest to see who can cut down the most trees in a day. The first lumberjack chops and chops and chops, never stopping, dropping tree after tree. The second lumberjack chops for a while, then stops and disappears for a few minutes. He does this several times throughout the day.

At the end of the day, the second lumberjack has cut down more trees than the first. The first lumberjack is astounded. **"How can that be?" he asked. "I chopped all day long without a break.** You didn't work near as hard as I did. What were you doing during your breaks?"

The second lumberjack replied, "I was sharpening my ax."

Evaluate your daily activities as either a) working on activities that are fulfilling and moving you nearer your goals, or b) renewing your physical, emotional, or mental energies—that is, "sharpening your ax."

Use the Pareto principle, or the 80/20 rule, when you evaluate your activities. To paraphrase this business principle, 80 percent of your results are achieved by 20 percent of your actions. (The Pareto principle is applied across a broad spectrum of concepts. For example, businesses derive 80 percent of their profits from 20 percent of their customers, and so on.) Think about what you do throughout the day, and decide which activities produce the most—and best—results. Then do those activities more often.

I've described how programming can lead you into doing things that go against your best interests. That programming can be insidious. You fail to question activities that need to be rethought. It's easy to fall into the trap of doing certain things because "We've always done it that way." Sometimes those actions are still valid, other times not.

A young bride cooked her first dinner for her new husband one evening. Before she put the ham in the oven, she carefully cut off the ends. When her husband asked her why, she said that her mother did it that way. She called to ask her mother about it, and her mother said that was the way *her* mother did it. The young bride called her grandmother and asked her why.

The grandmother replied, "When I was young, our roasting pan was too small for an entire ham, so I always cut off the ends so it would fit into the pan." Decide whether you're still using your grandmother's pan.

The Pareto principle illustrates the *tyranny of the trivial*. Trivial, non-essential activities can absorb your entire day if you let them. If 20 percent of your actions account for 80 percent of your results, what part of the rest of your actions can you eliminate without affecting the quality of your life?

Only a strict evaluation of how you spend your time will show you where you are most effectively reaching your goals. Leverage your time by spending more of it on quality pursuits, and you'll discover that you have "more time" than you had before.

### Decision making

We make millions of choices in our lives, sometimes without even understanding why. We have to learn how to connect our choices to our goals consistently and exercise those choices consciously. Often those choices are tough ones, because we want to do it all. Here are some steps to help guide your choices.

## FOUR STEPS TO EASIER DECISION MAKING

Ask yourself:

- Do I want to be, do, or have this?

- Will being, doing, or having this move me in the direction of my goal?

- Is being, doing, or having this in harmony with the laws of the universe?

- Will being, doing, or having this violate the rights of others?

If you answer yes to the first three questions and no to the fourth, the decision is made. Go for it. Practice answering these questions consistently, and you will soon find yourself making better and faster decisions.


## Don't spread yourself unnecessarily

There's an old saying: "If you want to get something done, give it to a busy person." Some people are able to shoulder the burden of getting a huge number of tasks completed. Usually these people have learned the art of *clustering*.

Clustering is grouping similar tasks together so that there is a minimum of wasted motion. For example, you might make all outbound phone calls at the same time. By doing this, you could have your address or phone book already open with the numbers you need, a list of all calls to be made (so you don't leave anyone out in the confusion), and a notepad and pen ready so you can take notes on the calls. Imagine if you had a large number of calls and had to reach for each of these items with every new call.

Other tasks, such as handling email or running errands, also lend themselves to clustering. Look at the time log you filled out earlier and see if you're spending an inordinate amount of time on mundane tasks. Are these tasks something that you want to spend a lot of time on, or are they part of the 80 percent that I discussed earlier?

What I'm talking about here is increasing the quality of the time you spend on tasks rather than increasing the quantity. While spending time on necessary mundane tasks can't be considered squandered, it's a waste of time to spend one minute more on them than is required.

## Say no

The quickest way to do tasks is not to do them at all. When you evaluated your activities, you probably found simple ones that may have appeared necessary at first, but after analyzing them, you determined that they weren't. Maybe they were outmoded or based on a practice that is no longer necessary. When you find such chores, deal with them decisively. Either find a way to get rid of them completely or find someone else to do them, someone who receives a benefit from their being completed.

Harder to say no to are those duties and responsibilities that might be rewarding but would take time away from another, more important, activity. Once again, you find yourself weighing the importance of conflicting desires. After considering your choices, say no to the activity that is less important, regardless of how rewarding it might be.

There is no need to feel remorse or regret after making such a choice. Life, after all, is full of good choices. (As a wise man once said, "You can have *anything* you want; you just can't have *everything* you want.") When the time comes to make such a decision, make it, inform the person asking of your decision, and move on to the more important task.

Since you are choosing wisely and thoughtfully, you don't need to explain or to apologize for your decision. Use courtesy, of course, but a simple statement such as "After giving it serious thought, I've decided for a variety of reasons to say no, but thank you for asking me" is enough for the other person to realize that you were honored to be asked, that you gave the matter some thought, and that you arrived at a reasonable final decision. Remember, "No" is a complete sentence.

For the sales professional, time is the one resource that you absolutely cannot afford to waste. Successful salespeople spend the bulk of their day actually in front of customers. They are either selling to customers, checking with customers to make sure everything is okay, or calling on potential customers.

It's been said that sales is the best-paying hard work and the lowest-paying easy work ever invented. There is a reason successful salespeople are among the highest-paid professionals in business. They work hard for their money. Sales is one of the few professions in which the worker directly affects, and immediately sees the results of, his or her efforts.

What's the difference between the highly paid, hardworking, successful salesperson and the salesperson who is starving? How they spend their time. While the successes are calling on customers, the starving salesperson is complaining about how bad business is or taking long lunches or otherwise making excuses for his lack of success.

Find tools and techniques that work for you. With the amount of technology available today, you could conceivably spend your entire day out in the field, talking to customers. The capabilities of modern cell phones alone are amazing. Use this technology to leverage the time you have available to you.

Although technology is wonderful, your most powerful tool is to ask powerful questions. Invest the time to remind yourself of your Big Goals and ask yourself strengthening questions such as, *How will I move myself toward my goals today?* Tell yourself that this is not about *Can I?* or *What's stopping me?* but about *How can I move forward?*

Remember, time is the most valuable resource you have. You can invest time and use it wisely, or you can squander it and wonder what happened to it. With few exceptions, you always have a choice about how you spend your minutes. *Take* the time to make the most of your time.

# CHAPTER 10
## FLOUNDERING AND FLAILING

GO AS FAR AS YOU CAN SEE, WHEN
YOU GET THERE YOU WILL SEE HOW
YOU CAN GO FURTHER.

–Thomas Carlyle

# CHAPTER 10
## FLOUNDERING AND FLAILING

Somewhere there is a perfect world where everyone lives in perfect harmony, where a pot of gold lies at the end of the rainbow, where trees are made of cotton candy, and all of the raindrops are lemon drops and gum drops, and plans always work out like they're supposed to.

Unfortunately, we don't live in that perfect world. We exist in our own imperfect world, where things not only can go wrong but usually do, and at the worst possible time (with a nod to Mr. Murphy). Although we may have perfect dreams and perfect aspirations, believing that we will reach all of our goals without any setbacks is not realistic.

Even the most successful people have setbacks. What they have learned, however, is to anticipate those setbacks and find ways to minimize both the damage they do and their duration. Successful people realize that the road to success is not a solid line but a dotted one. The spaces between the dots are the places where things can, and do, go wrong.

## The myth of the perfect plan

With all of the work that you've done up to now—determining your purpose and values, establishing a vision and mission, setting goals—you'd think that you would be able to see a plan through from start to finish without incident. Otherwise, you may ask, what's the point of all the work?

The answer is, because it would be even worse without the planning. No process is ever one hundred percent foolproof. Life is much too complex for any one person or group of people to anticipate every single possibility. If you don't believe that, watch the movie *Apollo 13*. The brightest minds in NASA, hundreds of scientists, worked for years to put a team of astronauts on the moon, yet that mission was scrubbed after an explosion in space. The mission at that point became simply to get the astronauts home alive. If that type of brainpower has to scramble because their plan went awry, a single human being can pretty much count on plans having to be adjusted somewhere along the way. But why?

First of all, you may have the *wrong plan*. Yes, it's true that if you have established your purpose, your values, your vision, and your mission, you are on the way to success. But it still might not be the right plan for you. Bad timing, an incorrect reading and interpretation of a situation, or a host of other errors in judgment can happen.

Trying to execute the wrong plan can be very frustrating and often means going back to the starting point and beginning anew. This fundamental change requires restructuring your viewpoint and reanalyzing your priorities. Forming the wrong plan means that you have been misled by some data that you took into consideration.

On the other hand, your plan may simply be *imperfect*. You may have the fundamentals down fine, but you've created a path to success that is unworkable, the usual reason for setbacks. You may have been overly optimistic or perhaps counted on results that didn't materialize.

The imperfect plan is immensely more preferable than discovering that you have the wrong plan. The wrong plan must be discarded and the entire process started over. The imperfect plan simply must be corrected and adjusted. The foundational elements of the imperfect plan are still valid.

Plans often go off track because of *imperfect information*. This can be information obtained from an outside source or something you believed to be true but that proved to be false. Without accurate information, of course, it's impossible to create a perfect plan.

Why do we use imperfect information when we create our plans? Sometimes it's all that's available. We can't always wait until everything is perfect before we get started, so we go with the best information we have. When we find out otherwise, the plan becomes imperfect. We have to make adjustments and rework the plan, incorporating the new information.

*)))* Sometimes plans go wrong because of our *assumptions*. Assumptions are beliefs that have no real evidence proving their truth. We may believe that we can count on a condition in the future because of our actions, without a real cause-and-effect connection.

An assumption that has thrown a plan out of whack recently is the mortgage crisis in the United States. It affected the world's financial markets and caused mass failings of investments and financial institutions. The entire mess is too complex to go into here, but one of the problems was with speculators who expected home values to continuously go up. The prices for homes had risen for several years, to sometimes astonishing heights. Money was invested—or gambled, more accurately—based on the assumption that real estate prices would always go up.

After the fact, of course, the tumble in real estate values and the following economic chaos seemed inevitable. Yet many financial experts based decisions on the idea of a never-declining housing market. This is a vivid example of an imperfect plan based on mistaken assumptions.

Closely related to mistaken assumptions, *mistaken beliefs* can throw off a plan. These beliefs are often the result of the programming we have received. It may be a belief you hold about yourself and your own abilities or about the outside world.

In either case, a mistaken belief that disrupts your plan is a fundamental problem and must be addressed before you can hope to make any progress. Mistaken beliefs lead you to make mistaken assumptions. If you formulate a plan based on the belief that a certain thing is true, you expect particular actions and reactions from taking steps in that plan. The wrong belief makes it impossible to anticipate the actual results of the steps you take.

## Are setbacks inevitable?

Given that we are all imperfect, and that an imperfect person cannot create a perfect plan, it's tempting to answer yes. Setbacks are a natural, normal part of life. However, it wouldn't be true to say that setbacks are inevitable. After all, sometimes plans go just as designed.

The answer to the question, then, must be that setbacks are not inevitable, but … Every plan will not suffer setbacks, but the vast majority of them do. It's simply the nature of the beast. Setbacks are common enough that experienced planners prepare for them. If you make enough plans enough times, however, you will inevitably encounter setbacks.

Another factor that is inevitable is *change*, and change is one of the things that can upset a plan. As Scottish poet Robert Burns wrote in "To a Mouse," "The best-laid schemes o' mice an' men, Gang aft a-gley." (For those who don't speak the Scottish dialect, Burns is saying, "The best-laid plans of mice and men often go awry.")

Change is everywhere in our world, from the momentary shifts in a breeze that determine a sailboat's direction to the adaptations that arise through evolution. We can't always predict exactly what change will occur or how it will affect us, but we can count on change itself. When we make plans, we base decisions and steps on the future we anticipate. When the situation changes, at least some parts of our plans are rendered inoperative.

If you set enough goals, eventually setbacks are inevitable. If your major desire is never to have a setback, then don't set goals. This is a major difference between people who work according to a plan, using goals, and those who simply stay busy, hoping for success.

If you never plan on attaining a certain level, then you can't suffer a setback. Whatever happens, happens. Only when you measure your progress, decide where you are, and compare it to where you want to be can you identify a setback. If you don't care where you go, it doesn't matter what direction you're headed.

Encountering setbacks means that you're *doing something*. Theodore Roosevelt put it this way:

It is not the critic that counts; not the man who points out how the strong man stumbles, or where the doer of deeds could have done them better. The credit belongs to the man who is actually in the arena, whose face is marred by dust and sweat and blood; who strives valiantly; who errs, who comes short again and again, because there is no effort without error and shortcoming.

Over a hundred years ago, Roosevelt recognized that the ones on the sidelines criticize the mistakes others make. The doers are the ones who make things happen, and things happen only through "error and shortcoming." While no one enjoys setbacks, encountering them means that you are in motion.

## Knowing when you're off track

Whether you call it a "setback" or "being off track," you must recognize when it has occurred. The key to identifying when things have gone wrong is awareness. When we talk about a person who is pursuing a goal, the image that comes to mind is that of the dogged and persistent laborer, head down against the elements, moving relentlessly forward.

That's not a bad image, and it's correct in some respects. However, anyone serious about achieving their goals needs to have their head up, looking around at the world to see what's going on. Sometimes missteps in a plan are so small that they don't even catch our attention. If the variance from the plan is gradual enough, we can be well down the road before we know something's wrong. By that time, the damage done may be severe.

Exhibiting constant awareness, however, means that you notice your environment and compare it to your expectations. The more quickly you can find a misstep, the more easily you'll minimize its damage. Corrections are also easier when the problem is addressed before it goes too far.

Part of the goal-setting process was to make sure your goals were measurable, one of the keys to noticing if your results are what you want. When results don't measure up, you know that something is wrong with the plan and that you are on course for a setback.

When all is said and done, of course, only results matter. You want to follow the process and remain true to your values, but at the end of the day, you depend on results to see how you're doing. Noticing your results is important if you want to aggressively attack errors in your plan.

Sometimes mistakes, or missteps, in your plan are very subtle, so logic and measurements may not be of use. Your subconscious mind will probably know something is wrong before your conscious mind does, and it will communicate to you the only way it knows how—through your feelings.

Have you ever been engaged in a project and felt that something was going wrong? You may become edgy and anxious for no reason or hesitate before taking the next step. Your feelings are communicating that something in the plan is out of alignment. Analyze your feelings when you reach this point, so you can take advantage of the subconscious mind's power to perceive things invisible to the senses.

The real test of a plan, however, is looking at it and asking the question, *Is this what I want?* Momentary doubts and second-guessing yourself are not what I'm talking about. I mean, when you come to the decision that your plan is not progressing as you wish.

You may have received new information that changes the entire complexion of your plan. If you plan to open a business in a particular location, the news that a competitor will open a week before you do, right across the street, makes your own plan problematic. You may have to change your plans. Only an analysis of the situation can determine whether your plan is actually what you want.

## What causes setbacks?

Again, one of the reasons for setbacks is that you are working on the wrong plan. The wrong plan can cause one disappointment after another, because what you hoped for never matches reality. Working on the wrong plan is a waste of time and energy.

Even when you have the right plan, however, poor execution can still cause setbacks. When you formulate your plan, you base it on performing at your highest levels. Then reality hits, and you're tired, distracted, or incapable of putting forth the required effort. In this case, the plan isn't the problem; the problem is you.

Before you descend into overwhelming despair at your deficiencies, you need to realize that nobody performs at the top of their game all the time. By definition, being at the top of your game means that at other times, you perform less effectively. It's not a crime, and it's not a sign of your incompetence. It's just the way things are.

However, don't base your plan on your deficiencies. You create a plan with the idea that you will be up to every task. On those occasions when a task gets the better of you, you experience a setback.

Even with the proper plan and proper execution, changing conditions can throw off the plan. The world is complex, and even things we normally count on can change. Without the benefit of seeing into the future, we have to base our plans on the way things are now, taking into consideration anticipated changes.

With the best of intentions and the highest level of competence, a plan can still be disrupted. Unexpected occurrences are, by definition, unexpected. No amount of planning or knowledge can anticipate everything that can happen. Everything from other people's decisions to acts of God can create an obstacle that is nearly insurmountable. When that happens, you experience a setback.

One example I used earlier illustrates the importance of one aspect of a plan—*timing*. Remember the plan to open a business but a competitor beat you to it? This event could fall into the category of unexpected occurrence, but it shouldn't. In business, competition is one of the things that we should count on the most. When money is to be made, someone will step in to make it.

Any number of factors can affect your timing. If you plan a big promotion on the same day another source captures the public's attention, you suffer from bad timing. Prudent planners look at their calendars when making plans, but everything depends on the individual steps. No one is able to anticipate every eventuality, and timing can cause a setback.

I hope you are getting the message that *change* is a huge factor in your success and that, once you manage change, your plans will meet with greater success. How do you go about managing change? I touched on one point earlier: your awareness of the world around you.

I've previously mentioned a mountain trail I hike regularly. There are bears in our area, and occasionally warnings are issued about them. I would be foolhardy to walk the trail when bears are around without paying attention to my environment. My plan to casually stroll up the trail would certainly suffer a setback if I had a close encounter with a bear. (For the record, I clip a bear bell onto my belt at such times so the bears hear me coming and can avoid me.)

Another way you can manage change is to thoroughly prepare before you begin execution of your plan. Although you can't make a plan completely foolproof, you can work hard ahead of time to minimize both the damage and the duration of missteps.

You can also use preparation time to address variations in your plan that may occur. Building safety plans have more than one emergency exit because planners know that the closest exit is not always available. Trying to defeat and resist change is a lesson in futility, but adapting to change and using it to your advantage is within your ability.

You can also control your *attitude* toward change. Of course, not all changes are pleasant, but they can create opportunities if you are receptive. If you agree with the notion that you perform better when you are happy and worse when you're miserable, you'll understand why your attitude about change is important to your performance.

When change is mentioned, we tend to groan, bellyache, and do everything we can to communicate our unhappiness at the prospect. What if you changed that mindset to one of excitement, anticipation, and eagerness to see how the change will affect you? If nothing else, you would eliminate the time you spend being miserable before the change even takes place. As a result, your performance will improve.

Another way to control how change affects you is to *be ahead of the curve*. In other words, be so prepared for the change that you actually look forward to it. By approaching change in this way, you have the advantage of being both physically prepared and mentally prepared.

You can have materials and information available when change happens, and at the same time, you can anticipate the changes with enthusiasm. When the change occurs, you can leap on it and use the new conditions to your advantage.

One of the causes of setbacks is what I call the *rubber band principle*. Any time you move out of your comfort zone, you "stretch" it. The further away you go from your comfort zone, the greater the pressure to return to your original state. As with the pressure from a rubber band, you're forced back to where you were.

Once again, old programming rears its head. Our motivators are to either avoid pain or pursue pleasure, and our programming associates pain with moving out of the comfort zone. We try to fall back into old habits and routines, the ones that got us where we are today.

The great thing about moving outside your comfort zone is that, just like a rubber band, you have to stretch to fulfill your role. A rubber band is useless unless it's stretched tight around something else. Your pursuit of your goals is only complete when you are stretching against your self-imposed limits, providing the goals are challenging enough and worth the stretch.

## Detours

Not all deviations from a plan are setbacks. Sometimes you have to take detours. The difference between a detour and a setback is that a setback moves you away from your goal. A detour, on the other hand, is a sideways move. It's a deviation from your preplanned path but not one that adds distance to your journey.

Although you decided on one route to success when you made your plan, it's not the only one. It may not even be the best one, but it's the route that you chose out of many. Circumstances may force you to scrap parts of your plan and make new arrangements, which may ultimately prove more productive.

Sometimes, the detour is not a complete change in plans but simply a delay, while conditions merge into the proper position. Sometimes plans will develop a bottleneck, where several factors compete for resources at the same time. At such times, you have to patiently work your way through the bottleneck to get things moving again.

It's hard not to view a delay as a setback, but unless you've missed out on other opportunities in the meantime, you aren't any worse off. The most difficult part of this situation is controlling your impatience. After you've developed momentum in your journey to success, hitting a temporary snag can seem like an eternity.

Remember that, unless a situation moves you further away from your goal, it's not actually a setback. What can move you further away? Repeating work you've already done is a setback. The second time around, you should be able to execute a step faster and better, but that's not always the case.

You can count on your patience being a little thinner when you are forced to repeat something you've done before. You have to be careful that your emotions don't turn a temporary delay into something much worse. Focus on the task at hand with the same diligence as you did the first time, and your new plan will be right back on track.

When you are forced to change your plan, carefully analyze your vision and mission to determine whether they are still intact. If either one of these factors has been corrupted, you have to decide whether it's better to scrap the entire plan and start over from scratch. Few things are as frustrating as discarding something you've worked hard to accomplish, but adaptability is one of the main factors in achieving success.

Bestselling author and success guru Bob Proctor tells the story of the time long ago when he had just finished writing a book and was carrying the completed manuscript on a trip. In those days of using typewriters, people didn't usually make copies of what they had written. Bob was no exception. As he arrived at one of his destinations, he realized that he had left the manuscript in the taxi. He was crushed when he was unable to locate it. Months of work were gone.

He had no choice but to rewrite the entire book. His thoughts were fresh in his mind as he began, and to his amazement, the second version was better than the first. In the end, losing the first manuscript resulted in a better final product.

Some of life's greatest gifts come to us through sadness and disappointment. Not until after the clouds have blown away do we see the many new possibilities all around us.

For a change to be considered a detour rather than a setback, you have to decide whether the goal is still achievable in some fashion, and whether you are still moving in the same direction. The goal is probably still achievable, if you are willing to adapt your plan to the new circumstances and embrace the new situation. Know your purpose, your vision, and your mission, and you will be on the right track.

## Getting back on track

If you don't realize that your plan has gone astray, you won't have a chance to correct it. For this reason, if for no other, you should occasionally take stock of where you are. Knowing that you have veered off course is one of the keys to getting back to where you want to be.

Look at what has happened. Before you completely change tactics, is there a way to get back to the original plan? You may have simply run into an obstacle that you have to go around. Be flexible in your thinking and see if you can find a creative way to return to your original intent. This option has the benefit of being able to use the resources you already had committed to the original plan.

If you can't get back to the original plan, is there a way to at least parallel the original plan? I mean not only in a physical sense, but also in a way that works along the same lines and principles. For example, you may have applied for a job that would be perfect for you and ideal to help you reach your goals. However, someone else got the job.

What do you do in such a case? Find another job that achieves all, or some, of the same goals. Success is sometimes achieved in large chunks and sometimes in smaller chunks. Don't let the fact that a large chunk escaped you prevent you from working on smaller chunks. Keep an open mind and accept the new circumstances. Adjust your route from your new location.

When you are forced to change your plans, is the new plan better? If you are open to change, you will often realize that your original plan lacked something, and that another way is more effective. You might have new information that opens the way for new methods, new approaches, or a new mindset.

## Setbacks as feedback

)) Remember that events are neutral, and that only our perspective and judgment label them as good or bad. You can use setbacks as feedback to help put you back on the right track. Adaptation is part of growing, and the ability to take new information and apply it to your situation is the mark of a successful person.

The famous story about Thomas Edison comes to mind. He tried 10,000 different materials to develop the filament for the incandescent light bulb. None of them worked. Eventually, of course, he found one that did, and modern society changed forever. When asked about the 10,000 failed attempts, Edison replied, "I didn't fail. I found 10,000 filaments that didn't work."

Use your setbacks as feedback that moves you closer to your ultimate goal of success.

# CHAPTER 11
## The Call to Action

> All of us are gifted; some just
> open our packages earlier than
> others."
>
> –Unknown

# CHAPTER 11
## THE CALL TO ACTION

As we approach the end of this book, it's time for you to clock in. There are no more delays, no more obstacles, no more excuses. Like any hardworking person, you know there is a time to go to work, and now's the time. You have the tools, you have the techniques, and you have everything you need to be successful. You are creative, whole, and *resourceful*—"full of resources."

)) Successful people know something that sometimes remains a mystery to the rest of us: *success is a habit*. It's not a door that you pass through, suddenly finding yourself in the "success room." It's the actual process of unlocking and opening the door, entering a room, and finding another door on the other side of the room.

Success is something you keep doing time after time. One of the lessons I've tried to communicate is that action is the only way to get something done. Through repetition you become more adept, because the skill of success is one that you can constantly refine and develop.

What's more, if you forget to practice the success habits, success will elude you. The principles apply universally, regardless of who you are. If you neglect your values or your purpose, you will not enjoy success.

For the sales professional, this point is vital. You must do something every day to improve your life, and you have the opportunity of doing so every time you encounter a customer. Repeat the success habits every day, and you will soon become proficient.

Another point is that you must use reinforcements to strengthen the habit of success. Associate with others who are on the same journey. Life is too short to try to convince naysayers and negative thinkers. Read motivational literature, listen to inspirational speakers, find a mentor, and attend classes and seminars that focus on success.

Remember to read your goals aloud twice a day. This simple act reinforces your commitment to success and to work as hard as necessary to become the best at what you do. This reinforcement comes from within. When you reinforce your own success habits, your subconscious mind—the wild pony that it is—begins to submit to your will and work for you instead of against you.

Finally, remember to reward yourself for your successes. Make the reward appropriate to the success—small rewards for small successes, larger rewards for larger successes. Rewarding yourself is not self-serving, nor are these intermediate rewards the reason for the work you do.

When you reward yourself for a particular action, you associate pleasure with that action. The mind, as we know, motivates you either away from pain or toward pleasure. You can use fundamental psychology to make your success a habit.

While the bulk of the message in this book has been directed toward the businessperson, and particularly the professional salesperson, the principles can be applied throughout your life. First of all, consider the different roles you assume during a typical day: parent, sibling, employer or employee, coach, mentor, protégé—the list is very long.

Now take each role and create a vision for that role that aligns with your values. Do you think you have a particular purpose you were meant to fulfill because of that role? Go through the process to create goals and objectives for each of your roles to maximize the amount of success you can enjoy in each.

Unbridled ambition is not appropriate for every role you fulfill, however. You may be completely happy being the parent of a child in soccer, with no desire to be the coach. Within that role, how can you define success? Is it with spending quality time with your child, helping him or her develop their skills, watching them compete? The definition for each person will be different, but the process is the same.

Keep your core values in mind as you consider success and goal setting in your various roles. Above all, you want your goals to be worthy and your success to fulfill you on every level. Worthy goals accord with your values. Violating your values to achieve shallow success will only leave you empty and full of regret.

Remember that success is based on action, and you can't sit around waiting for success to "happen" to you. If you wait another moment to get started, you'll have wasted that moment and will never get it back.

Throughout this book, I've worked hard to help you find the answers to the questions asked at the beginning. How do you find answers? Be aware of and accept your current circumstances and environment. Use what you learn to create a plan that will take you to the next level of success. Work from your most basic values, stay true to those values, and respect the values of other people. Develop the traits of trust through transparency, authenticity, advocacy, and integrity. Whether in your personal life or in sales, you'll be on the right path.

As George Burns said, "I look to the future because that's where I'm going to spend the rest of my life." And it doesn't hurt if you laugh and have fun along the way!

)

## CHEERS!